COLLECTION
*Gratianus*
SERIES

Wi.

2009

W&L
WILSON & LAFLEUR

# OTHER BOOKS
# BY THE SAME AUTHOR

- *Introducción al estudio del Derecho Canónico*, EUNSA.

- *Lecciones propedéuticas de Filosofía del Derecho*, 3ª ed., EUNSA.

- *Historia de la Ciencia del Derecho Natural*, 3ª ed., EUNSA.

- *Cuatro Lecciones de Derecho Natural*, 4ª ed., EUNSA.

- *Una Caro. Escritos sobre el matrimonio*, EUNSA.

- *Escritos de Derecho Natural*, 2ª ed., EUNSA.

- *Los eclesiasticistas ante un espectador*, 2ª ed., EUNSA.

- *Coloquios propedéuticos sobre el Derecho Canónico*, 2ª ed., Navarra de Ediciones.

- *Elementos de Derecho Constitucional Canónico*, 2ª ed., Navarra de Ediciones.

- *Vetera et Nova. Cuestiones de Derecho Canónico y afines (1958-1991)*, 2 vol., Servicio de Publicaciones de la Universidad de Navarra.

- *Pensamientos de un canonista en la hora presente*, 2ª ed., Navarra de Ediciones.

- *Pueblo cristiano y circunscripciones eclesiásticas*, Navarra de Ediciones.

- *Vetera et Nova. Cuestiones de Derecho Canónico y afines (1958-2004)*, 2ª edición remodelada, Navarra Grafíca Ediciones.

## TRANSLATIONS

- *Introduction to the Study of Canon Law*, Gratianus Series, Montréal, Wilson & Lafleur, 2007.

- *Critical Introduction to Natural Law*, Gratianus Series, Montréal, Wilson & Lafleur, 2006.

- *Introducción crítica al Derecho Natural* has been also translated into Italian (ed. Giuffrè), French (éd. Biere), Portuguese (ed. Res Jurídica) and Hungarian (Szent István Táriulat).

- *Elementos de Derecho Constitucional Canónico* has been translated into Italian with the title *Diritto costituzionale canonico*, ed. Giuffrè.

- A wide selection of "Una Caro" has been edited by ed. Giuffrè with the title *Studi sull'essenza del matrimonio*.

COFOUNDERS
ERNEST CAPARROS
MICHEL THÉRIAULT (†)

# What is Law?

## The Modern Response of Juridical Realism

### An Introduction to Law

Javier HERVADA

Translation by
William L. DANIEL

2009

Bibliothèque et Archives nationales du Québec and Library and Archives Canada cataloguing in publication

Hervada, Javier, 1934-

What is law?: the modern response of juridical realism: an introduction to law (Gratianus)

Translation of ¿Qué es el derecho?

Includes bibliographical references.

ISBN 978-2-89127-910-9

1. Law – Philosophy.  2. Law – Spain.  I. Title.

KKT440.H4713 2009   340'.1   C2009-941199-7

Spanish edition: Pamplona, 2002
© Copyright 2007, Javier Hervada
Javier Hervada: E-mail: jhervada@unav.es/http://www.unav.es/canonico/j.hervada

© Copyright 2007 for the English language translation Wilson & Lafleur Ltée, Montréal (Canada)

*Nihil obstat quominus imprimatur*, Marianopoli, die 15º maii 2009,
Michaël Parent, P.H., I.C.L., vicarius episcopalis, cancellarius, Censor deputatus Curiæ.

*Imprimatur*, Marianopoli, die 15º maii 2009,
Ioannes Claudius cardinalis Turcotte, archiepiscopus Marianopolitanus, N.P. 6/2009

Legal Deposit, 3rd quarter 2009
Bibliothèque et Archives nationales du Québec
Library and Archives Canada

Orders to:
*Canada & International:*
*Wilson & Lafleur Ltée*
40, Notre-Dame St. East
Montréal (Québec) Canada  H2Y 1B9
Tel.: 514 875-6326 / 1 800 363-3227
Fax: 514 875-8356
*www.wilsonlafleur.com*

USA:

*www.CanonLawBooks.com*
2662 East Allegheny Avenue
Philadelphia, PA 19134-5115
Tel.: 215-634-2355
Fax: 215-634-2373

*Midwest Theological Forum*
1420 Davey Road
Woodridge, IL 60517 U.S.A
Tel.: 630-739-9750
Fax: 630-739-9758
*E-mail: mail@mwtf.org*

ISBN 978-2-89127-910-9
Printed and bound in Canada

# Table of Contents

# Editor's Presentation

Each book has a history. And the translation of this great little book by Professor Javier Hervada has a very interesting one.

Some time ago, Professor Jane Adolphe, from Ave Maria School of Law and a member of the Gratianus Editorial Board, informed me that one of her students, Mr. Reed H. Allen was working on an English translation of the original Spanish *¿Qué es el Derecho?* That a law student in a school located in Ann Arbor, Michigan, had discovered the book was a surprise to me, and I was delighted to learn that some English-speaking persons had shown interest in Hervada's thought.

After speaking with Professor Adolphe, I agreed to consider whether Mr. Allen's translation could eventually be published. However, many other publication projects occupied my time and I did not turn my mind to Hervada's book again until I spoke with Mr. William L. Daniel.

While working on a collection of decisions of the Signatura Apostolica to be published in the original Latin accompanied with an English translation, Mr. Daniel and I spoke on various occasions about canon law. He demonstrated a very good knowledge of Spanish and a great interest in the Lombardía-Hervada canon law school of thought, in particular in Hervada's writings. As a result, I asked him to consider translating Hervada's book and gave him a copy of Mr. Allen's translation to assist him in determining whether he could take on the project.

I knew that Hervada's writings presented serious challenges due to the differences in legal vocabulary between the Latin and the Anglo-Saxon languages. Indeed, certain nuances in the writings of Professor Hervada were in some cases very difficult to appreciate and capture, as Mr. Daniel admits in his Introduction where he outlines the many challenges.

I edited Mr. Daniel's translation, comparing it with the original, occasionally modifying some of the terms or expressions in order to better manifest Hervada's reflections, in the hope that my efforts would benefit English-speaking readers.

I am grateful to many people: first of all to Mr. Daniel who took on the project and prepared a very accurate and readable translation, and to Mr. Allen, now an associate attorney in Aurora, Colorado, and Professor Adolphe for their collaboration. And in a very special way many thanks go to our copy editor, Madame Johanne Paquette, who did a meticulous job, reading and suggesting amendments. Last but not least, I am indebted to Mr. Claude Wilson, our publisher, and his team, for all their support and wonderful work.

Ernest Caparros
Editor
Montréal, 23 March 2009

# Translator's Introduction

While the meaning of the term "law" may strike the English-speaking ear as evident in itself, jurists would observe that the word is multi-faceted and even at times ambiguous. For instance, using the same term, one can refer to a specific traffic law, to Civil Law, to the "law of the land," and to divine law; however, the word "law" is being used here in substantially different ways. Respectively, it refers to a particular human regulation governing a focussed aspect of one activity in the purview of the government, to a whole human legal system, to the normative expectation of society, and to the will of God regarding human life. Similarly, in the canonical context, a specific canon is or contains a law; the canonical system is called Canon Law; canonical customs are part of what is called customary law (cc. 23–28); and canon law is subject to and in some places articulates divine law.

This conceptual distinction is enshrined by two separate words in every other major modern Western language, as well as in the mother tongue of the Latin Church. In order to refer to a system of law, to any normative rule, or to the divine law, the following words are used: *ius* (Latin), *derecho* (Spanish), *diritto* (Italian), *droit* (French), *Recht* (German), *direito* (Portuguese), *prawo* (Polish). For example, these terms are used in the title for the *Code of Canon Law* in each language: *Codex <u>iuris</u> canonici*, *Código de <u>Derecho</u> Canónico*, etc. In order to refer more specifically to a legislative norm, the following words are used: *lex* (Latin), *ley* (Spanish), *legge* (Italian), *loi* (French), *Gesetz* (German), *lei* (Portuguese), *ustawa* (Polish). Such a nominal distinction is not found in English. How then can one coherently respect these conceptual distinctions in English?

In order to refer to a system of law in English, one can use simply "law" or "system of law." The word "law" or "norm" can be used to refer to any standard of conduct or regulated relationship or structure, whether they are from God, the Church, the State, an institution or commonly expected practice (custom).[1] When referring to a specific prescript within such a system promulgated by a legislative authority, expressions such as the following can be used: "law," "legislative norm," "legislation," or "piece of legislation." The use of the word "law" to refer to any one of these concepts should not normally pose a problem when its meaning is clear from the context. The problem arises when the

---

1. In the canonical system, the English word "norm" (like the Latin *ius*) can also be used as a general word to refer to all kinds of generally binding rules: legislation (*lex*), general administrative norms (c. 32–34), customs (cc. 23–28), statutes (c. 94), and rules of order (c. 95).

words are found in close proximity to each other or when they are actually being compared.[2]

This problem is highlighted at the outset of this translation of Prof. Javier Hervada's *¿Qué es el derecho?*, because, as one might expect from the title, it arose frequently in the translation process. The reader may be able to detect this in many places. Here is an example from Chapter I, Section 3 (emphasis added in bold):

| | |
|---|---|
| Jurista es, sencillamente, el *hombre de* **derecho**, el hombre que sabe derecho. También se dice con frecuencia que es *hombre de* **leyes**. | A jurist is simply *a man/woman of* **law**, a person who knows law. It is also frequently said that he or she is *a man/woman of* **laws**. |

In this translator's judgement, it was not suitable to use any term other than "law" in both cases since the expression *hombre de leyes* recurs throughout the work and is more intelligible than "man of

2. For similar discussions, see Ernest CAPARROS, "Presentation of the English edition," in Javier HERVADA, *Critical Introduction to Natural Law*, Gratianus Series (Montréal: Wilson & Lafleur Ltée, 2006) xi–xiii; Amleto Giovanni CICOGNANI, *Canon Law*, 2nd ed., Joseph O'HARA and Francis J. BRENNAN (trans.) (Westminster, Maryland: The Newman Press, 1949) 9–12; John M. HUELS, *Liturgy and Law. Liturgical Law in the System of Roman Catholic Canon Law*, Gratianus Series (Montréal: Wilson & Lafleur Ltée, 2006) 64. For an historical approach to the problem, see Charles J. REID, Jr., "Thirteenth Century Canon Law and Rights. The Word *ius* and Its Range of Subjective Meanings," in *Studia canonica* 30 (1996) 295–342, esp. 299–301.

legislation" or the like; also, the plural form of *ley* sufficiently distinguishes "man of laws" [*leyes*] from "man of law" [*derecho*]. In this and in similar places, we insert the Spanish term for the sake of clarity.

Another problem altogether lies in the opposite phenomenon: whereas English has separate words to refer to objective *law* (the meanings discussed above) and a subjective *right* (something that is due a person), the other languages mentioned above do not; in every case, the primary word used for "right" is the same as that used for "system of law" or "norm" (the Latin *ius*, the Spanish *derecho*, the French *droit*, etc.). In English, we can use both concepts in the same sentence without any confusion: "The right of association is established by the law." In Latin, though, the same word is used for both "law" and "right": *Ius consociandi a iure constituitur*. Similarly in Spanish: *El derecho de asociación se constituye en el derecho*. The same is true of the other languages.

An example of this problem in the present book is seen in Chapter II, at the end of Section 2 (emphases added):

| | |
|---|---|
| Por cierto que, después de decir que el jurista es hombre de derecho, hemos descrito su saber como la ciencia de lo justo. ¿No es esto un ejemplo de incongruencia? | Certainly, after saying that the jurist is a man of law, we have described his knowledge as the science of what is just. Is this not an example of contradiction? |

| | |
|---|---|
| El saber del jurista ¿es la ciencia de lo justo o la ciencia del **derecho**? No hay que precipitarse en pretender descubrir incongruencias: lo justo es justamente el **derecho**; decir *lo justo* es nombrar al *derecho*, porque son lo mismo. Cuando, por ejemplo, decimos que es **derecho** del arrendatario ocupar el piso alquilado, estamos diciendo que esto es lo justo, supuesto el contrato del arrendamiento. Correlativamente, si se interfiere o ataca **un derecho**, decimos que eso es injusto. Lo injusto es *la lesión del* **derecho**. | Is the knowledge of the jurist the science of what is just or the science of **law**? One should not hastily try to discover contradictions: what is just is precisely **the law**; to speak of *what is just* is to refer to *the law*, since they are the same thing. For example, when we say that a tenant has **a right** to occupy a rented apartment, we are saying that this is what is just in view of the tenant's contract. The corollary is that we say it is unjust to interfere with or attack **a right**. What is unjust is *the harming of rights*. |

In order to refer to norms (found in a code, a contract, etc.) and rights in Spanish, the word *derecho* must be used; but English has the benefit of two separate terms. Hence, we are able to say that the tenant's **right** (*derecho*) to occupy a rented apartment is established in or supported by some **normative source** (*derecho*). (This problem with the word *derecho* is directly dealt with by the author at the very beginning of Chapter III, and it is again cited at the beginning of Chapter V, Section 2.)

It is my aspiration that the reader will be spared any confusion because of these linguistic problems. If at any time my efforts inadvertently give way to a misrepresentation of this eminent jurist's thought, I take exclusive responsibility. I do hope that my translation is successful in conveying the humility, gentlemanly manner, and supernatural outlook of this thinker; for these are evident in the original text.

I am grateful to Professor Ernest Caparros, the editor of the Gratianus Series, for having supplied me with a draft translation prepared by Mr. Reed Allen, Esq. Since Spanish is not my mother tongue, his draft proved to be a useful resource when I found certain expressions ambiguous or when they escaped me altogether. It was also delightful to work with Professor Caparros on this project, and I am grateful to him for his encouragement, professional demeanour, and good humour.

William L. Daniel, JCL
Translator
March 2009

# Foreword

This book is an introduction to law. This means that, for the most part, it is directed both to people at the beginning of their study of law (be it in a faculty of Law or in a faculty of Canon Law) and to those who are already experienced jurists or canonists who wish to recall or review the foundations of their craft.

In a certain sense, then, this is a rudimentary book, but it is far from being a publication for the general public. For this reason I have intended to be clear, but I am not guaranteeing that it will always be easy reading.

Moreover, I dare say that this is no practical introduction. It can be classified as original in some ways. It is an introduction to law from the perspective of classical juridical realism (understanding law [*derecho*] as what is just). Although it is a perspective as old as the Roman jurists, at the beginning of the 14th century it was practically replaced by subjectivism (understanding law as a subjective right), and then by normativism (understanding law as a norm), which is still the dominant perspective today. For this reason, returning to juridical realism is an attempt at renewing and modernising the juridical science. It is not a view toward the past, but a purification of the science of law from a frail and antiquated vision, which has sufficiently demonstrated its own sterility and the deforming effect it has had on the work of the jurist. In this sense, this book can be considered a synthetic and propedeutic exposition of classical juridical realism—a method that is different from the usual way of learning law. For this reason I believe this book can be of interest to jurists and canonists alike.

Of everything that is said in this introductory book, I think it most important that this idea be well illustrated: the final, fundamental goal of the science of law is that a society may be just, with that real and concrete justice that consists of respecting and giving to each person the rights that are his or hers. This task is important and of incalculable social transcendence, even though achieving it may at times require great efforts. It is a task in which it is entirely worthwhile to persist.

Pamplona, 9 January 2002

# Chapter I

# The Whole Truth About
the Study of Law

## 1. Introduction

There is something unique about the study of law with respect to other courses of study. If a medical student is asked what he is going to be when he completes his studies, he will undoubtedly respond, "A physician." It is true that some who study medicine will not practice medicine—that is, they will not be dedicated to seeing and curing the sick—but they will be dedicated to other activities related to medicine, especially research. I know a prestigious researcher, a professor in a faculty of Medicine, who tends to get angry when someone introduces him as a physician or asks him what to do in order to cure such and such an illness. His invariable response is, "I am not a physician." Such situations are exceptional. A faculty of Medicine teaches its students how to be physicians; and although it is true that it is not prudent to expect a recent graduate to treat a patient—it is better to wait for him to acquire some experience—it is no less certain that the graduate in Medicine has the basic knowledge needed in order to be a physician. The same is true of other studies, such as Architecture or the different branches of Engineering.

On the other hand, if one asks a law student what he intends to be upon completing his pro-gramme of studies, one can receive a multitude of responses—as many *opportunities* as these studies have, exceeding a hundred. The student might even shrug his shoulders and, to the astonishment of the inquirer, respond, "I do not yet know what I am going to do."

What does this mean? Is the study of law sim-ply a conglomerate of disciplines that have little connection to each other? Or could it be that it teaches a little bit of everything? If this were true, then the saying "man of many disciplines, master of none" would apply to graduates in law. Experience, however, tells us quite the opposite: graduates in law are found among the highest-ranking in the range of professions, from politicians to diplomats. A law programme does not teach many trades or disciplines; it teaches one trade or discipline that truly qualifies a person for a great diversity of careers.

At least a few years ago, there were many who thought that a faculty of Law teaches one to be *a law-yer*, which would be the craft or discipline which we are talking about. This conception about a programme of law has only one minor disadvantage, and this must be very clear: in faculties of Law one is not taught to be a lawyer; among other things, *dialectics* and *rhetoric*, which are two essential arts for the lawyer, are absent from the curriculum.

Regarding the study of law and what is taught in a faculty of Law, one should know the whole truth ahead of time: in a faculty of Law, a person is going to learn how to be *a jurist*. Nobody is alarmed by this reality; what is meant by the name of jurist is the knowledge or art which will open doors to a multitude of professions, more than any other curriculum. Some professions consist of being simply jurists—jurists *par excellence*, like judges or magistrates; others represent certain facets or derivations, such as being a lawyer or a notary; and others are professions for which it is necessary or fitting to be a jurist: a diplomat, a politician, or a civil servant.

## 2.  Being a jurist

What is meant by the term "jurist"? This word comes from Latin, the language of the Roman jurists, who were the ones to transform knowledge of law into an art or a science. In Latin the law was called *ius* (or *jus*; the letter *j* is nothing more than a lengthened *i*); hence, the term "jurists" meant those who are dedicated to the law (to *ius*), just as soccer players are professionals in soccer, and artists are those who are dedicated to art. The reader may understandably think that, since the word *derecho* [law] is used in

Spanish, it would be preferable for jurists to receive a name derived from this word so as to avoid confusion. In fact, in the Middle Ages, when Spanish began to take form, this intention already existed, but the word that resulted was *derechurero*, which still appears in some dictionaries; they called justice *derechuría*, and so it happened with other words derived from *derecho*. It is understood that *derechurero* and *derechuría* were soon forgotten, and today we gratefully follow the good sense of our ancestors, speaking of jurists and justice.

## 3.   Man/woman of laws

A jurist is simply *a man/woman of law* [*derecho*], a person who knows law. It is also frequently said that he or she is *a man/woman of laws* [*leyes*]. This second expression, *man/woman of laws*, is more understandable for non-specialists, and not a few jurists are convinced that it is better. These jurists are called *normativists* since they assert that the law is legislation (also called *a norm*, whence comes *normativism*). In the pages which follow, we will see that legislation [*ley*] and the law [*derecho*] are not the same, but normativism is the dominant conception of law.

These differences in the very notion of law are not to be surprising, since one's notion of law depends on one's notion of the human person and of society. Our society has become so pluralistic that we make people call into question even these most basic ideas.

Nevertheless, what we intend to do in this book is to demonstrate precisely that law is not confused with legislation, nor is the jurist properly a man or a woman of laws, even though it is of primordial importance for him or her to have knowledge of laws.

Having arrived at this point, it is our concern to proceed to an explanation of the components of law and consequently of what it is to be a jurist.

# Chapter II

# Why the Art of Law Exists

## 1. Knowing the law is a practical science

Knowing the law, understanding it, is a practical science. It is very common today for one to have a rather reduced concept of *what is practical*. People call something practical when it has an immediate usefulness: for example, money, pleasure, consumer products, one's workplace, or (in a more extreme form) what is useful for structural reform or social revolution. This is *what is practical*, while what remains are *theories, philosophies*, or, in a less academic expression, *stories*. With this more restricted sense of what is practical, it becomes difficult to understand what one means by saying that knowing the law is a practical science. It is not surprising that there are students who complain that at times their professors' explanations are scarcely "practical." That which is not directly useful for preparing for their exams or competitions, for winning arguments in future lawsuits, or for settling their taxes is an *abstract* and excessively theoretical matter; what is necessary, they say, are *practical* classes.

Personally, I am convinced that *there is nothing so useful as un-useful things*. Nothing has more utility or is so helpful for being fully actualised in life as the wisdom which comes from metaphysics—the most abstract and the least "practical" part of philosophy, which is scarcely "practical," to say nothing of religion which decides humans' eternal destiny. However, I am not going to go in this direction. If we measure what is practical by its immediate usefulness, there is no doubt that the study of law is very practical since it offers many professional opportunities, and it is the one least affected by unemployment, though it is not immune from it. Nevertheless, when we say that knowing the law is a practical science, we are not speaking in this sense.

## 2.   Determining what is just

It is said that the sciences—or systematically organised disciplines—are speculative or practical in a sense which has little in common with the sense of the *practical* to which we just alluded. The word "speculative" comes from the word *speculum*, or mirror; it refers to a knowledge which reflects reality without making it or constructing it. If a person is dedicated to the study of art, he will attain knowledge of the paintings of artists studied in their most minute details; it can happen that he knows all or almost all of the paintings, from the materials which the painter used as paints to the direction of each one of the brushstrokes. All of this, though, is speculative knowledge; this knowledge will not qualify a person to paint if he does not have *the art of painting*. This art consists of knowing how to paint pictures, and it is a practical science. A practical science and an art are the same thing; art is the whole practical science and not only what are called the Fine Arts. It is clear, then, that it is one thing to know paintings (speculative science) and another to know how to paint them (art or practical science). A tennis critic, who knows how to distinguish a good stroke[3] from a defective one, can be incapable of correctly holding a tennis racquet. What then is an art or a practical science? It is *knowing how to do* various things.

On the other hand, in order to know how to do something, seemingly useless knowledge is often necessary—that is, knowledge that is not immediately practical. A very clear example is mathematics. Mathematics is a speculative science, and it is among the most abstract: nothing immediately happens with mathematics; nothing new has been done after an arithmetic operation; a piece of data is simply understood. Even placing written numbers on a piece of paper belongs to the art of writing, not mathematics. Nevertheless, there are very few things that can be done without using mathematics. As was said before, nothing is more useful than what is "un-useful." Speculative learning—which contains little or nothing practical—is also necessary in order to know the law; but law is essentially an art

---

3. Translator's note: The author gives an example in the context of bull-fighting. His point is more easily understood, though, by citing a more common sport.

or a practical science. And what practical thing does a jurist know about? He knows about something so fundamental and important for social relations, namely, *that which is just*. The jurist is dedicated to being restless about what is just in social relations, in society; he is, in a manner of speaking, *a technician of justice*, knowing what is just and what is unjust.

There is probably some reader who senses a surge of scepticism or protest in the face of these assertions: who knows what is just? All of this about what is just seems more like politics than law. Moreover, if a certain kind of jurist should come to read these pages—namely, those whom we call normativists—he would say that this is too pretentious; it is sufficient for the jurist to investigate what is legal and illegal. Nevertheless, we have already said that those who had the art of knowing the law were the Roman jurists; and one may suppose that they who performed such a great feat with respect to the law knew it rather well. On the other hand, it is known that the Roman genius was eminently practical, scarcely given over to speculations and utopias. In any case, the Romans are the ones who defined the art of law as *the science of what is just and unjust*. Perhaps justice and what is just end up being less pretentious and utopian than they seem, and knowing what is just may not be more or less difficult than investigating what is legal. Or it may be that justice is sufficiently less proper to politics than one would think, given the frequency with which politicians use and utter that cliché, "a just and solidary society."

Has justice not been idealised? It could be that we have confused the common chicken within everyone's grasp with a golden pheasant. The jurist is the one who knows whether justice is not this utopia which is proper to "the elite of the world" or something much more within reach than "the just and solidary society." There is something suspicious about saying that the Roman jurists had a more utopian and idealised sense of *what is just* and *what is unjust* than our contemporaries seem to have. For, as all historians say, the Romans are known for their *practical* genius; they did not bequeath great speculations, but (because of their practical genius) they made a decisive contribution to Western civilisation: the art of law or the science of what is just.

Certainly, after saying that the jurist is a man/woman of law, we have described his or her knowledge as the science of what is just. Is this not an example of contradiction? Is the knowledge of the jurist the science of what is just or the science of law? One should not hastily try to discover contradictions: what is just is precisely the law; to speak of *what is just* is to refer to *the law*, since they are the same thing. For example, when we say that a tenant has a right to occupy a rented apartment, we are saying that this is what is just in view of the tenant's contract. The corollary is that we say it is unjust to interfere with or attack a right. What is unjust is *the harming of rights*.

Perhaps with this brief clarification it can be perceived that justice and what is just are not so utopian as they seem, except to the extent that we understand law to be a utopia.

## 3.   Why law exists

For the moment, however, let us set aside the fact that law and what is just are the same, and let us now begin to explain what justice and law are. In order to do this we have to return to the foundation and origin of law by reducing the problem to this question: why does law exist?

In order to respond to this question, it may be useful to state it in another way; while not being identical, the following question may lead us more simply to the answer: why has the art of law arisen?

Every art corresponds to a need. Sometimes the needs are those that are called *primary* or *basic*; and so there exist what are called items of basic necessity. On the other hand, there are needs which we humans have created, which we could get rid of with a little common sense or simply by being more temperate and sober. In any case, though, just as an art consists of knowing what *to do*, knowing how *to produce* and the like, it is clear that every art arises in order to satisfy a need. This depends on the realities and factors of human life. And so it is with law.

What is the need which the art of law satisfies? On what social reality or factor of human life does it depend?

In the first place, lest we get lost in a jungle of opinions and be led astray, we are going to restrict ourselves as precisely as possible to that aspect of human life which is proper to the jurist. Take note that we are not dealing with the politician, the citizen, or Parliament. Jurists are judges, advocates, attorneys, prosecutors, notaries, etc. Members of Parliaments, governors, premiers and prime ministers are not jurists (the art of law is not the function proper to them, although they may perhaps possess it by having studied it). If we wish to restrict the art of law to the functions and powers of the State, we will not include Parliament or the legislative authority, the government or the executive power; we will turn to the judicial power. In effect, judges and magistrates are jurists; their task is to exercise the art of law. It is also exercised by those who have an immediate connection to the judicial function. If the task of the judge is the resolution of controversies, those who pursue the controversy before the judge as *counsellors* of the parties are jurists as well, namely, advocates and the public prosecutor.

As a more representative example of the art of law, let us concentrate on those who intervene in the trial. The rest of the professions or duties are nothing more than variations, insofar as they are juridical.

What does the counsellor of the *petitioner* do, that is, the counsellor of the one who makes a petition (a claim) before the judge or court? It is said that he presents a claim of justice; fine, but what does he request? It is clear that he does not make his argument in terms of a "just and solidary society"; the reader should bear in mind that those who argue in this way *do not have recourse to judges*. They have recourse to Parliament, to public opinion, or to the government. When one approaches a judge with a claim of justice, the terms are much more modest and, if you will, prosaic. The judge is asked to declare that the inheritance of X belongs mostly or partially to Y, who is the petitioner; or that A owes B a certain quantity of money and that he is consequently obliged to pay the debt; that C has the right to pass through D's land (or his field; this is called a right of way, an easement); that the mayor of city E has exceeded his powers to order the demolition of a building constructed by F; etc., etc. What is being requested? The request is simply that the judge issue a sentence, which declares with authority what belongs to each one of the parties in the judicial process. (A sentence is a declaration, and deciding is equivalent to declaring.) It is requested that he decide or declare that a certain part of the inheritance of X belongs to Y, that a certain quantity of money must be handed over to B by A, that the mayor of E does not have the power which he has usurped, etc. Even in trials where the request is only the comparison of two laws—e.g., the unconstitutionality of a piece of legislation—what the judge will definitively say in declaring the unconstitutionality of a law is that the one who prescribed the law lacked the power to issue a law contrary to or irreconcilable with the constitution. The judge decides or declares what belongs to each one; it is a sentence about *what belongs* to each. The advocate, too, states and defends what he believes is his client's (what belongs to his client), although, without lacking professional ethics, he endeavours to defend the most favourable solution. The task of the public prosecutor—and that of other jurists, in one form or another—can be described in the same way. On the other hand, in reality, there are no *purely* juridical offices, that is, those solely and exclusively dedicated to the function of the jurist. The judge also moderates the process, he makes provisions and orders, and he commands the execution of the sentence; in some cases this is entrusted to the registrar.

The object of the jurist's knowledge is *that which is one's own*, what belongs to each one. We have called each one's possession—what belongs to someone—*a right*, the right of each person; to discern what is "one's own" (what belongs to each one) is to discern what his rights are. The art of *one's own* (what belongs to each one) is the art of law. And just as the jurist is not a benefactor, a patron or a miser, what he discerns is not that which is convenient for each one, what is pleasing to each one, what each one desires, or what is possible, or anything else whatsoever, but his right—nothing less, nothing more, but exactly that which is ascribed to him; the jurist indicates the just thing that must be done to each one. Therefore, *what belongs to someone*, *what is just*, and *rights* are three ways of referring to the same thing.

## 4.   Allotment of things

With this, though, we have departed from the original question. We were intending to identify the need to which the art of law corresponds or the aspect of social life to which it owes its origin. The aspect of social life to which the art of law corresponds emerges from what we were just explaining. If there are things which belong to one person or another, if they are *their* things (those of each one), if rights and what is just pertain to determined subjects, it is clear that this is because *not everything belongs to everyone*—or, said in another way, that *things are allotted*.

Some have said that this phenomenon is due rather to *a scarcity of things*, which is what makes humans fight for things and necessitates that they be ascribed to some people and not to others. This position, though, does not seem correct to us. For example, even if there were an overabundance of food and everyone could have as much as they should want, each person would *take possession* of a determined amount—soon, the food would be allotted. The fact that no one would complain about his portion only means that there would not be disputes and, in the general plan of everything, that there would not be courts, just like there would not be lawyers, etc.; but this does not indicate the disappearance of rights. We can propose another example: an overabundance of automobiles. What would happen if no automobile were ascribed to anyone because of overabundance? Each citizen, upon leaving his house, would seize the first car that he came upon and would go to his workplace; to return he would do the same. For the moment, it seems to be an ideal situation, were it not for some minor details.

For instance, what would one do with the luggage he is carrying if, instead of returning home, he had to go directly to the airport to catch a flight? Since nothing would belong to anyone, there would be no problem: were someone to take the car with the luggage, he would seize the first piece of luggage he could find, and he would take the accessories which others may have left here and there (remember: the goods are assumed to be overabundant)... Why continue? This would not be paradise; it would be a madhouse. *What is one's own*, the attribution of things (a right) does not derive from a scarcity of things but from something else: humans are prompted within the dimensions of quantity and space, and it happens in the same way with the things that serve them. In another respect, humans are finite, and human society implies an allotment of functions and tasks (everyone cannot simultaneously be the head of State, governor, colonel, judge, baker, plumber, etc.). Human life demands that *things*—goods, functions, burdens—*be allotted* and, consequently, attributed to distinct subjects; hence, there is mine, yours, and his or hers.

If things are allotted, *everything is not everyone's*, and this is a social necessity. Let us suppose that everything is everyone's. If this were the case, money that one has to cover his expenses could be snatched by another; then it would belong to both of them. If a person's body were to belong to everyone, a sick person with two unhealthy lungs could be treated by seizing a healthy person's lung and transplanting it for one of the sick man's lungs. If houses were not attributed and allotted, everyone could invade the house that he desired whimsically, etc., etc. Human life would be hell. The normal development of human life insists that there be a certain attribution of things, that not everything be everyone's—at least in the sense of respecting the harmonious use of things. However, there may be a lesser degree of attribution; for instance, if a citizen is seated on a public bench, another citizen cannot throw him off just because he sat on it. A person can at least say that, while he or she is seated on a public bench, the ability to sit there is something that is his or hers; it is attributed to him or her, and therefore it is his or her right.

The non-attribution of everything to everyone is a social necessity which results in the fact that things are allotted. And in order for things to be allotted, there are rights. Where there are rights, there exists the art of law.

From what has been said, it follows that the necessity which supports the art of law is among those which are primary or fundamental. The law is a *basic necessity*.

# Chapter III

## Justice

### 1. A just social order

We have already indicated that rights arise from the fact that things are allotted. That which we have been calling a right [*derecho*] is a *just thing*, a thing attributed to a person. It would not be right, though, if we failed to observe that the name law [*derecho*] is also given to legislation, according to the way languages are translated; this is the linguistic phenomenon in virtue of which we use the same word in order to designate two mutually related things. For instance, we say "radio" in order to refer both to the company which emits radio programmes and to the receiving apparatus; or a "café" is the place where one goes to drink a cup of coffee [*café*].

When law [*derecho*] is taken as legislation [*ley*], we are not dealing with the allotment of things but the *ordering of conduct*. The originating act is not allotment but the ordering of human activity; in effect, then, the proper function of legislation is the rational ordering of human conduct. It must not be forgotten, though, that ordering or regulating social life according to rational criteria is proper not to the jurists but to the people in governance. Hence, legislation is not issued by judicial organs; it is issued by political organs: Parliament, the government, or the people themselves by custom, plebiscite or referendum. Issuing legislation is an art which corresponds to politicians; it is part of the art of politics, which is responsible for constructing society according to justice, freedom and solidarity.

If the jurist articulates which social conduct is ordered, he always does this in relation with the order established by nature or politics and to the extent that the conduct is what is just—that is, it pertains to the realm of freedom or of someone's obligation: to act or not to act in a specific manner, according to what is just in relation to another or to a social body. Ordering social conduct is properly a political art. Hence, it is necessary to insist that the key concept of the art of law is that of *allotment*, not order. However, one might object: is it not said that the goal of the art of law is a *just social order*? Yes; in effect, the goal of the jurist's art is a just social order. Well then, what is intended by the expression "just social order"? Not, of course, utopias and political practices, but some condition of society in which each person has what is his or her own and may use it without interference; but here the key concept continues to be that of allotment.

## 2. Justice

We have repeatedly spoken of justice and of what is just, and a moment ago we referred to the just order. What then is justice?

When faced with this question, normativists usually show themselves to be somewhat negligent; it could be said that the question troubles them. This is not surprising. Attempting to define justice on the basis of norms—as the value and original dimension of legislation—is time lost. Whenever one has attempted to define justice from the perspective of legislation—and some attempts come from Greek Antiquity—he has ended up constructing a new tower of Babel. In recent times more than 200 definitions of justice have appeared, to the point that one can detect an increasing amount of scepticism about the notion of justice. Hence, the perspective has been skewed. Justice is not *primarily* an effect of a norm; it does not arise from legislation; and therefore it is not the primary (proper) dimension of politics. Justice *is conferred upon* politics and therefore legislation; and they thereby become law [*derecho*] (they are considered just things). It is not something primarily *required* of legislation and politics. Hence, the ability to understand justice is impeded by making all law derive from legislation. Since justice depends on law, and therefore only if some law that pre-exists legislation and the art of politics is admitted, justice can be introduced into legislation and politics. We

will return to this point later; for the moment, these
initial observations are sufficient.

## 3.   Giving each his own

We recall that the Roman jurists transformed the
knowledge of law into an art; they defined justice as
*giving to each one his own*, and also *giving to each one
his right* [*derecho*]. Both formulae are identical, since,
as we were saying, one's own and one's right are the
same thing.

This definition contains nothing utopian, imprecise or empty of content. Much less is it absurd or
tautological like what some philosophers or theorists
of law (normativists) have attempted. It is highly
*practical* and *realistic*; it is filled with content; and if
one wishes to find some defect in it, it will be that it
does not represent an ideal or political Messianism.
For supporters of a "just, free and solidary society,"
this formula is colourless, odourless, and tasteless.
On the other hand, it is refreshing for the jurist and,
above all, for the multitude of citizens who live with
daily realities and not with ever-unrealised, grandi-
ose ideals.

Despite some confusion, justice (giving each
one his own) is as practical as the daily work of
judges and the rest of jurists; it is so realistic as to be
attainable for every person of good will. And it is so
rich in content that Aristotle said of this virtue that
it was more beautiful than the light of the morning
star (this kind of expression is not common in the

mouth of an ancient Greek man). And Dante—expressing a fact from experience—affirmed that, if justice is protected, human society is preserved; and if it is neglected, society is corrupted. This justice, which appears so modest and grounded (it seems to lack great spiritual heights), is the justice whose fruit is peace, so longed for by persons of all ages. When is there peace except when the rights of each person, each community, each people and each nation are recognised and respected?

If this seems somewhat impractical, unrealistic and lacking in content to some of our contemporaries, it is because it is necessary that one possess a secret, inasmuch as it joins the simplicity of its formula with the very important results that are attributed to it. The formula has a trick. Aristotle was in possession of this secret, as were the Roman jurists and jurists in general, until the *positivists* appeared in the 19th century—that is, those who deny that human beings have rights inherent to their condition as persons. For this is a secret, an evident truth which became hidden by those who place the veil of positivistic obscurity over the juridical science. (Positivism is one of the more subtle forms of being voluntarily blinded from the light.) Indeed, the secret is *natural law* [*derecho natural*]. If it should happen that some reader has not heard of natural law, and as it is not now the moment to explain what it is (we will do so at a suitable time), I will limit myself by saying that a natural right [*derecho natural*] is every right which each human being has in virtue of his or her nature—his or her condition as a person. That is, it is the entirety of the person's own things, his or her rights, which he or she has in him or herself and not by concession of Parliaments, governments or society: his or her life, his or her physical and moral integrity, his or her natural freedoms, etc. Perhaps the reader is thinking that these are human rights. Well, for the moment we can accept this comparison; when one devotes several years of study to these matters, he will then be capable of distinguishing what is common and distinct between natural rights and human rights.

The secret or trick in the definition of justice lies in natural law, because without natural law only the rights given by human laws remain. And so justice—consisting of giving each one his own right—could be reduced to giving the human person these rights; and no one objects to this. So notorious are the insufficiencies and injustices which are ushered in by so many human laws that no one can admit that justice is reducible to this—besides Marxists, for whom justice is a product of the bourgeois. Natural law is the secret, because the insufficiency and injustice of legislation are judged by their correspondence with natural law, which is a law as concrete as *positive* law (which owes its origins to the concession of society); therefore, the whole potential contained in justice is *concrete*, practical and realistic. In contrast, if natural law is neglected or rejected, justice in relation to natural law becomes empty or is changed into a collection of vague and relative ideals; the definition of justice will have lost its practicality and realism. Let us not disturb the definition, though, with positivism's defects.

## 4. Justice follows law

Now that the nature of justice has been established—the virtue of giving to each his own—it is fitting to focus in on some of the details. The first of these can be stated by means of a proposition which is self-evident. Nevertheless, it ends up being scandalous to those who hear it—which justifies Saint Thomas Aquinas, when he says that propositions that are self-evident are not always evident for everyone. And they are not evident when the terms of the proposition are not wholly understood.

The proposition to which I allude is this: *justice follows law* [*derecho*]; it does not precede it, but it is posterior to it in the sense that it operates in relation to existing law. Why is this proposition self-evident? Inasmuch as every proposition is evident: because it is contained in the definition of justice. If justice is the virtue of giving each his own (his rights), in order to be put in motion, it is precisely necessary that someone's "own" (what is *his by right*) exists. If not, how can we give someone what is his own, what is his by right? One would have to give him something else. Therefore, wherever there is no existing right, justice cannot be invoked. This is elementary. Let us propose an example. If an employer and the employees of a company have agreed upon

a monthly salary of $1,200, to whom will the employ-
ees have recourse if the employer gives them only
$720? They will have recourse to a judge, and he will
order the employer to give the employees what is
theirs (their right), which is $1,200. And for that mat-
ter, if it is necessary, he will sequester the employer's
goods. What if the labourers make a protest before
the civil government instead? With abundant grounds,
the governor will tell them to have recourse to the
courts. In paying only $720, the employer commits
an injustice.

Let us now consider the opposite situation. A
contract fixes a salary at $720 per month, and the
labourers appear before the judge and request that
he order the employer to raise the salary, arguing
that there is an increase in the cost of living. The
judge will be inhibited; the question is not within
his competence since the labourers have a right
to $720, while they wish to receive $1,200. The
means for obtaining a raise in their salary is a new
contract, a labour strike, a syndicated action, or a
public demonstration. Their aspirations are not
questions of justice but policy. No one can *seriously*
invoke justice in this case since there is no basis
on which the *strict* right of the labourer—that which
is just, neither more nor less—is a salary of $1,200.
If there were some provision foreseeing automatic
salary adjustments—e.g., a clause of common agreement or a legal disposition—then it is clear that justice would intervene, and it could be brought before
the judge.

We can ask, though: are not humans' *aspirations just* in the proper sense? One can have them, but in such a case we are concerned with true rights. Discerning rights is the function of the jurist; and in the event that they are not respected, the judge can and must intervene. Do they not do so? Sometimes there are judges and jurists who are deficient in their function or are unjust, at least in part. If they are not personally unjust (formal injustice), they are at least bound to a system that protects and applies a law that contains injustices.

When the aspirations are true rights, and justice consequently intervenes, it is obvious that one is dealing with rights that pre-exist and precede positive law, that is, natural rights. With this we encounter the theme of unjust legislation. Without a doubt there is unjust legislation; there are things that are unjustly attributed (we can understandably call these rights). This, however, only means that justice pre-exists positive law, the law issued by humans, not that it pre-exists any law. In other words, unjust laws exist—indeed they exist! They are unjust, though, *because they violate natural law*—either because they attribute things to persons who are not the proper recipients designated by natural law, or they deny someone's entitlement to a thing which he has in virtue of natural law, or they attribute things to persons who have been denied them by natural law.

To summarise, if unjust law [*derecho*)] exists it is not because justice precedes law, but because there exists a natural law that precedes positive law, which the latter cannot debilitate or nullify. Or, to say the same thing in other words, justice precedes positive law as a consequence of the existence of natural law.

## 5.  Equality

Justice is commonly represented as a blindfolded matron holding in her hands a balance with the two plates in perfect equilibrium. The blindfold and the levelled and motionless beam of the balance are two symbols of the fact that justice treats everyone equally.

Equality! It is a magical and mythical word in our time. The political cliché about a "free, solidary and equal society" returns to view when justice is perceived as equality. Here it is also necessary to know that the cliché begins to unravel. The need to unravel the cliché is well understood, not because such a society is not a worthy goal to fight for. (Of course, we are not dealing with this since the present book does not address policy.) Freedom, solidarity and equality can be values to which one might worthily commit himself, if they are correctly understood. Moreover, they are goods and values especially dear to the jurist, since, beyond being the support of more progressive juridical systems, they summarise the more important aspects of natural law. Then what is the problem? It is problematic that the cliché "free, solidary and equal society" is a political *slogan*, and few things are so damaging to the art of law as confusing and intermingling it with politics.

The equality of justice is not the equality to which egalitarian politicians aspire. In current political terms, equality at times refers to the aspiration to give *the same thing* to everyone. At least in some matters, this is an aspiration upon which we can look with sympathy in the political sense (we are free to do so); but we must be very clear that this *is not the equality of justice*. (We do not mean that this is always unjust; we simply mean that it is a political aspiration, not a demand of justice.) What is the equality that is proper to justice? It is something that is contained in its own definition: to give to each his own. All are treated equally, since all are given what belongs to them.

Perhaps the reader is feeling somewhat disappointed; the equality of justice seems to be demystified and down-to-earth. Might it be unjust (in the strict sense of justice) to eliminate clamorous and bloody social differences? Is the just thing being pursued when, in these situations of tremendous inequality, each is given *his own*—what is declared by property titles, what is established by governmental decrees and stable situations of privilege? This avalanche of questions is good, but it would be better not to rush forward too quickly. I already said that there is a trick to the notion of justice—understanding justice like the Roman jurists, and no one can find anyone more convincing—and this trick is natural law. It is perhaps that, in the cases to which the questions refer and in virtue of natural law, the titles, the decrees and the privileged situations are

less firm than they seem, and they do not attribute
things as much as it appears. Perhaps if jurists interpret positive law in light of natural law (instead of
being stuck in positive law like positivists), they
would allow it to have a dynamic element and move
in the direction of a more just society. Of this I am
convinced, but I do not mean to treat this now. What
is interesting to consider is that the equality of justice
appears demystified and, for this reason, it is feasible
and possible in each time, place and situation; one
need not hope in the triumph of a political faction or
the transfer of power to some political redeemer.

The primary aspect of the equality of justice is
represented by the blindfold: justice does not
discriminate; it is not prejudicial to persons. Said
in another manner, justice is not *fixed to a person*;
it is fixed exclusively to each one's rights. It is not
more attentive to the rich than to the poor; it does
not assign occupational positions on the basis of
favouritism; it does not decide on the basis of recom-
mendations; it is not attentive to sympathies or
antipathies; it does not have a double standard, etc.
What we are saying here is sufficient for perceiving
how much just behaviour is lacking in our world
and how much the jurist can do. Racial discrimination and apartheid, discrimination on the basis of
sex, nationality, birthplace and any other form of
prejudice against persons are injustices. On the other
hand, this state of things *does not leave one hoping in
the decisions of politicians* if jurists apply the *law*,
which is not only positive law but also natural law.

These situations are unjust, and it is in the hands of jurists (especially judges) to change them; it is enough that they propose change. If jurists are placed in proximity with forms of discrimination with the excuse that the laws are thus established by humans, they are inexcusable and disloyal to their art or function, unless they themselves are victims of an unjust system.

The other aspect of equality, represented by the weight of the balance, is that justice—as we said before—does not give the same things to everyone, but it gives each one his own (the weight which is placed on one plate must be the same as that placed on the other in order for the balance to have equal weight). At first blush this perhaps does not seem to be equality, but it is. Let us recall a classic example. In a hospital or clinic, are the same treatments and medicines given to all the patients? Or is each one given the medicine which his illness and organic reactions require? It is evident that the equality which we all desire is the second, and we desire it because the first is simply absurd. The reader may draw his own conclusions. That which is just is treating everyone equally insofar as they are equal and differently insofar as they are different—but *proportionally*; this is the key. There thus emerges an element that corrects the exaggerations of egalitarianism, which is a form of injustice. To give each one what is his own is the precise expression of just equality: equal treatment in that which is equal and proportional treatment in that which is different. In this way can one appreciate how wholesome it is to demystify the equality of justice; in its practicality and realism, this equality is what places human co-existence on solid foundations.

## 6.   A minor detail

It should be noticed that justice demands that what is one's own be given *to each one*. This is a minor detail about a matter that is not usually favoured with commentary, as if it were an unimportant issue. How often, though, do people wish to call attention to it! I do not know if the reader has observed the facility with which this "minor detail" is forgotten by certain political and social movements which have justice as their banner and mission statement. The collectivist mentality has so strongly permeated our society that there is an effort to apply justice to large blocks, social classes and groups, while the individual is neglected.

What is important about the person in comparison to the interests of the masses? There are outcries and struggles for the justice of one's countrymen, for one's people, and for such and such a group of marginalised people. If the pursuit of the "just cause" that is being defended requires the "liquidation" of "oppressors," can one deny that this is only a "people's" justice? Does the life of the oppressors have any importance? If one's "revolutionary duty," abduction, terrorism and assault are necessary in order to obtain justice, can all of this be justified since it is done for "the cause of justice"?

The manner in which this mentality is presented is often more subtle and "civilised." And so, there is talk of the need to overcome the contrast between freedom and equality (justice, as we have seen). It is said that, when it is not possible to obtain both, it is necessary to sacrifice freedom (and with it certain individual rights) on the altar of a more just and equal society. What is important is justice for the social class, for the people, for groups and communities.

This, of course, is not what is just, nor can such ways of thinking and acting be attributed to justice. On the contrary, these actions proceed from injustice. To speak of justice in these cases is a manipulation of the term.

There thus emerges the minor detail of giving *to each one* his right. Of course, justice concerns society as a whole. We saw this earlier in the words of one of humanity's greatest poets: protected, justice preserves society, and its destruction ruins it. Justice, however—which endeavours to build up society— gives *each one* his right, person by person, individual by individual, community by community. It is like those great painters capable of making gigantic paintings—not with great brushstrokes, but detail by detail, point by point. It is, we might say, a punctilious virtue. It does not lie with outlines; it does not reside with the common people, a social class, or a group: it builds up society individual by individual, person by person. It sees human dignity in each person; in each person one contemplates a being necessarily endowed with rights—the image and resemblance of God—and attention is given to each person. And so justice asks for patience, while injustice is the vice of the impatient.

This is why justice, which is also a virtue of politicians, is not left to politicians for fulfillment. Politicians usually prefer great plans and celerity in obtaining the fruits which come from the patience of justice. In every minimally organised society, control over justice and the function of guaranteeing it is placed in the hands of the judicial power. This power does not act by means of large guidelines or more or less ambitious schemes. It listens to the citizens *one by one*, controversy by controversy, trial by trial. It takes each person into account, issues a sentence for each case, and protects each citizen. This is justice: to give to each one his right.

Hence, this "justice of the group," which does not fail to attack the rights of individuals, is nonsense. We have called it by its proper name: it is a hypocrisy which conceals injustice.

This "minor detail" of justice, though, also carries a message for jurists. The art or science of law is not ultimately a science of concepts, systems, and general theories. Neither concepts, nor systems, nor general theories are of service if they are not at the service of what is just in each case. They are of service if they assist with the disclosure and declaration of what is just in each concrete social relationship. They are detestable if they bring rigidity to the resolution of cases, if they obscure what is just rather than disclose it.

## 7. Justice and allotment

While it may only be a preoccupation of mine, it is possible that at this point a question may be circuiting the mind of someone who has had the patience to read thus far: if justice consists of giving each one his right and rights pre-exist justice, how does one give to someone what he already has? If he has it, how is it given to him? This same question was posed by one of the greatest philosophers, Kant. It is not prideful, though, for this hypothetical reader to ask coincidentally the same question as one of the better-known intellectuals. Just as all of us humans err, when the most intelligent are confounded they are at times accustomed to pose the most absurd questions. And, with all due respect, this question is an example of a mental "slip." This question gave Kant a basis for saying that the definition of justice which we have been developing—to give to each his own—is absurd; but the one who fell into the absurd was him.

In effect, justice does not consist of *creating or consenting to rights* but of *giving* that which pertains to them *when they have been interfered with or injured*— that is, to return, restore, or compensate. In order to consider the definition more precisely, let us consider that a right is *a thing* which receives its name in the measure in which it is attributed to a person. For instance, my *property* (my property right) is the house which I buy or receive by inheritance; the eventual use of the public park for walking by is my right, as is the money which I possess. Also, the titular of rights can cease to be in control of his things (rights). For example, a friend could ask me for a loan—let us say five dollars; these five dollars continue to be my property, and yet they are not now in my power but in my friend's power. It is clear that my friend does not have a right to the five dollars that I have loaned to him; it is an act of friendship on my part. It is not a gift (a donation) but a loan; my friend owes me these five dollars. *To give them to me,* to return them, will not be an act of friendship but of justice. When, after a qualification exam, the State *gives* me possession of the position that I obtained through the exam, it is performing an act of justice.

And so it is not a matter of creating or consenting to a right but of *giving that which corresponds to a right*: respect, a return, compensation, restitution, etc. The act of creating or consenting to a right—which presupposes its prior inexistence—does not belong to justice but to authority and power. The act of creating and establishing a right is a *primary act* with respect to justice and, prior to that, the act from which the right originates. On the other hand, as Pieper says, justice is a *second act*, because it presupposes the first act which establishes the right. Hence, for God as The Creator of human beings the act of creation, just like the benefits which are received from Him, is not an act of justice toward humans; the action of God with respect to humans comes from love and mercy. It is the same with parents: the collaboration by which children are engendered does not fulfill an obligation of justice toward them but of love, which gives way to a debt of gratitude.

This point supports what we were saying about the basic fact to which the law corresponds: things are allotted. Justice is realised in relation to an allotment already made; but making an allotment—assigning things to distinct subjects—is not proper to justice: *justice does not primarily allot things*. And this affirmation is self-evident, since it is contained in the very notion of justice. This can be surprising, though, since we fully acknowledge that there are things which are poorly allotted and unjustly distributed (this is evident), and therefore we coherently aspire for a just allotment to be made. This is certainly true, but let us return to what we discussed before: if the actual allotment of goods has unjust aspects, this is due to the fact that we humans have allotted the things in violation of some pre-existing rights, namely, those which make up one's natural rights. This supposes that there are things which are already allotted by nature—in virtue of natural law. Hence, the new allotment will not be the *first* redistribution but the *second*. This new allotment, this redistribution, will be a work of justice to the extent that there are natural rights; and in this case, a second act will occur.

If there is an actual unjust allotment of goods and a just redistribution is requested, one of two things can happen when one's natural rights are denied: either there is some point of inconsistency, or there is an intention to substitute what is just with ideologies. In both cases, justice is harmed.

In order to further clarify what we have just said, let us propose an example. If person A, who has no legal or natural obligations to his possible heirs, allots his goods by will among B, C, and D, this allotment is a *first* allotment. In so doing, A does not exercise justice, since there is nothing due his heirs. Once A dies, the goods, which were already allotted *de iure*, will be *de facto* allotted among B, C, and D, in accord with the will; this allotment, which accomplishes the wishes of the deceased, is done in justice, but it is a *second* allotment.

If in establishing the will A had certain legal, natural or contractual obligations with one of his heirs, his allotment, with respect to these obligations, will not be the first one but the second one, because earlier the portion of the inheritance affected by the obligations was already assigned to the respective heir. In this aspect, therefore, A was acting justly in fulfilling his obligation. It will always trace back, though, to the first allotment (which is made by a law, custom, agreement or natural obligation), which is not proper to justice. Justice regarding what is one's own does not allot things, but it presupposes an allotment already made by nature, human law, or an agreement.

## 8. What belongs to each—neither more nor less

The final aspect of justice to consider is that which concerns *what is one's one*. Justice gives to each one what is his own, neither more nor less.

There are two comments that can be made about this point. In the first place, the fact that justice gives what is one's own reminds us (once again) that justice presupposes that what is given already belongs to someone—that it is the right of the one to whom it is given. Rights pre-exist justice. We have already sufficiently spoken about this, and it is not necessary to return to what was said. As a friend of mine would say, "it is a sufficiently published thesis."

Still, it is worthwhile to pause somewhat for our second comment. Justice does not consist of giving each one what he needs, what leads to happiness, to development, etc. Justice gives each one what is his own, and no more—and also not less, since that would be an injustice.

The conclusion which is hence deduced is that it is nowhere seen that the "just society" is an ideal of society, nor that justice can be a longed-for goal which brings happiness to humans. If we understand ourselves correctly, society collapses without justice. For this reason, it is certainly necessary to fight so that a society may be just. And among the means available for this fight is the art of law; and those who are most able and obliged to ensure that justice is introduced are jurists—but they are not the only ones. A society that is *only* just, however, is an intolerable society. If a person is only given what is just, there would be no friendship, no affection, no generosity, no help, no solidarity, nothing that allows for the normal and adequate development of social life. Hence, the just society and justice are points of departure, not political *goals*; they are the principle and the base, not the ideal.

Justice is to the society what a concrete or steel structure is for buildings. Without a structure the building will not be maintained; but with only a structure it will be not fit to live in. Without justice, society is destroyed; but with only justice it is intolerable.

Is this a new demystification of justice? Yes, because it is necessary to be realists and to found one's action in the truth. Justice is not some ideal, but a foundation; it is a principle, not a goal. Can one be committed to justice? Of course, but all of us humans have this commitment, since justice is an obligation (a commitment) which is a basic necessity; it is not a special ideal. It is like someone having the opinion that no one should be assassinated. What an opinion! Well, we can say the same of the commitment to justice. What a commitment! My, what a society in which being just seems to be something special, something capable of justifying a particular commitment; this would be an unjustly organised society, that is, lower than the least. It is not justice that justifies a commitment but love for humans.

Love, fraternity, giving to others with self-sacrifice: these are commitments which it is worthwhile to assume—the highest, if this love for humans has its roots in the love of God. Justice is the minimum to which we are all obliged in relationships among humans; and the minimum cannot be an ideal.

# Chapter IV

# Rights

## 1. Clarification about subjective rights

These pages have not been written principally for jurists but for those who wish to become jurists and also for those who wish to take time for a brief reflection on the law. If some jurist is reading this book out of curiosity, though, perhaps he is thinking that I was mistaken in my description of rights on the previous pages. I have written that a right is a just thing or a thing that is due in justice. I have said that the house which belongs to me, the use of a public road, the ability to travel freely, the money I have at my disposal (very little, which is why the example of the loan which I proposed was no higher than a modest five dollars), bringing a claim before the courts, etc. are *my rights*. If the curious jurist does not wake up to juridical realism, or if he has been educated in normativism, he will probably feel called to correct me: the house is not a property right but its object; said otherwise, he would have to say that I have the property right *over* the house. The right of using a good is not the use itself, but the *right to use* it, and so it continues. In other words, at each step I have been confusing a right with its object.

There is no such confusion, though. A right, "one's own," and what is just are the same, identical things; and what belongs to each one, what is just (one's right) are *things*, corporeal or incorporeal things. The right *over* or the right *to* something is not the right of which I have been speaking, but that which is called *a subjective right*.

A subjective right is a faculty to do, omit or demand something. It is said that it is above all a faculty to demand. For many jurists—from the 19th century to the present—a right is not a *just thing* (which would be the object of the right) but the faculty over or in relation to the thing. So for instance, a property right over a house would be a complex of faculties: that of demanding its restitution if it is illegally inhabited, of selling it, of destroying it in order to construct a new house, of living in it, etc. Well then, are these faculties? They undoubtedly are; but, from the standpoint of rights, they do not form their own category as so many jurists have understood since the 19th century; they are not a new form of being for rights, and much less do they displace the just thing as a right. These faculties are rights because they are *just things*—they are the titular's possession inasmuch as they derive from the principal fact, established by being the titular's *property* (following the example), which is a type of right. In other words, a subjective right is not a right to the exclusion of being also a just thing.

I considered it reasonable to make this clarification for four reasons. First, in order to defend my reputation: I am not confused. I understand the modern doctrine of subjective rights; I simply do not share it. Rather, I believe that the juridical science must correct the perspective from which it considers subjective rights.

Secondly, I am being loyal toward any future students of law who read these pages. They may hear much being said about subjective rights, and it is therefore fitting to allude to them in this introduction.

The third reason is so that I may contribute to the cause of the marginalised. Subjective rights—which were given thrust and vitality in the 14th century by the spiritualism of the English friar William of Ockham, who wished to be so poor that even his food could not be called his own by right—are an open trap for the individualism of the 19th century to numb the consciences of the powerful with regard to the poor. In effect, if a right belongs to a person (radically, a subjective right), the right exists insofar as one has a *moral faculty*, regardless of what is possessed in reality or when one has nothing over which to exercise it. For example, the freedom to enter a contract is recognised for every labourer. Well, it happens that a labourer finds himself in a situation of inferiority with respect to the employer when it comes to discussing his salary on account of the need to work and the scarcity of opportunities—as would happen at the end of the 18th century and the beginning of the 19th century; hence, he would tend to accept the inadequate salary that was offered to him. *This results in indifference toward one's rights.* Just as rights consist of *formal* freedom (that is, the simple moral faculty), the freedom to enter a contract is already recognised. (Hence, laws do not impose a salary, nor is an act of physical coercion exerted upon the labourer.) Another example: the law recognises the freedom of education. Soon this becomes financially prohibitive, but *this is not a juridical problem* according to the doctrine of subjective rights. Every person's right to health is equally recognised; if a person does not have money and cannot buy the necessary medication, it is a misfortune that will have to be alleviated by charity; but it is not a problem of justice. And so it goes *ad infinitum.*

Juridical realism rejects such a conception of rights as false and unjust. Just as a right is not primarily a moral faculty but a thing that is due, the freedom to enter a contract is accorded the labourer and the employer when it places them in a situation of discussing the terms of the contract on an *actual* plane of equality and without coercion. (It defends the labourer as well as the employer before the coercion of labour unions; we recall that justice does not discriminate.) Similarly, the right to education is recognised when the State helps parents and educational institutions decently maintain the teaching centers created for them (it does not appear otherwise in the current circumstances). And everyone's right to health is recognised when remedies are placed within the reach of all.

In order for a right not to remain on the merely theoretical plane, bringing it into reality is a *juridical problem*; stated otherwise, we assert that this is a problem of justice. And this constitutes the task of jurists, among who are judges. Since a right is not simply a moral faculty—since there are moral faculties which are not rights—jurists and, among them, judges must interpret laws in practice; this concerns rights not in a formal sense but rights in the real (or realistic) sense. In accord with this interpretation, it must be made in the playing out of concrete circumstances; it is not acceptable to be stuck in merely formal interpretation. For instance, if the constitution recognises the freedom of education, it is incorrect to admit as constitutional a law that *permits* the creation of educational centers and simultaneously *impedes* the State from granting the pertinent assistance. Laws which govern supermarkets must be interpreted such that food may be within everyone's reach—to be nourished is a natural right of every human. And if it happens that a restored market economy leads some to suffer hunger and others to have an overabundance of food, such laws must be the object of a corrective interpretation on the part of jurists. On the other hand, a labour strike is a right of wage earners, but the interpretation must be made such that, by defending their rights, there is not unjust coercion by the managers, etc., etc.

The fourth reason is simply that rights are the object of justice; and what justice *gives*—respects, restores, compensates—is things.

## 2. External things

As we have repeatedly said, a right is a thing which is due to a person in justice in virtue of it being attributed to him.

Since we are now more particularly analysing rights, the first thing one should understand is what type of things can be rights. In principle, the word "thing" has a generic sense, which indicates that the realities which can constitute a right are of a very different nature. They can be material things (*res corporales*) such as pieces of property, houses, agricultural produce, artistic objects, clothes, etc. They can also be immaterial things (*res incorporales*) such as positions, powers, faculties, etc.

Nevertheless, all of them must have a common characteristic: they are things that have an external dimension (*res exteriores*), which, in themselves or their manifestations, spring from the intimate sphere of the subject. The reason is obvious: since justice consists of *giving* that which pertains to a right, someone's possession could be an object of justice only if it can be an object of everyone else's activity. What remains in the sanctuary of the conscience and of a person's thoughts, that which dwells within the private realm of secrecy, does not enter into a relationship with others and, consequently, is not an object of the virtue of justice.

## 3. The reason for indebtedness

A thing becomes a right by its condition of *debt*— when indebtedness in the strict sense falls upon it. It could be thought that this affirmation is imprecise, since a debt and a right seem to be contrary things. It seems better to say that a thing is a right since it is attributed to a subject independently of the fact that another owes this thing to the subject. For example, my lighter is my right as much when I have it in my power as when another to whom I have loaned it owes it to me.

In order to understand this aspect of rights, it is necessary to recall that a thing is a right—not from the perspective of dominion but from the perspective of justice. Robinson Crusoe, a solitary on an island, undoubtedly had a series of things that were his; but in that situation rights had no reason to exist. To say these things were his rights would be entirely useless. When would those things begin to have the purpose or character of rights? It would begin when Friday appears and then when Robinson enters into relationships with other persons. In effect, at first it would have been useless to speak of rights; but at the moment in which Robinson enters into relationship with Friday, the things which Robinson has

made his own *must* be respected by Friday. In the
perspective of justice, things attributed to another
appear as debts. This characteristic *colours* things
which receive the name of "rights" because of their
relationship with the subject to whom they are
attributed. It is rightly observed that justice is not
the perspective of the titular of the rights vis-à-vis
the things attributed to him, but it is the perspective
*of others* vis-à-vis these things; and before other persons, what emerges is the indebtedness of respect,
restitution, compensation, etc.

In this sense, my lighter is my right both if it is
in my power and if I have loaned it. If it is in my
power, though, it is my right inasmuch as others
must respect my dominion over it. If I should lose
every possibility of being in relationship with others, I would continue to have dominion over and
use of the lighter, but calling it a right would be
effectively meaningless. Magpies, monkeys or other
animals could rob me, but rights are not at stake
with respect to animals.

Precisely because rights take their origin from
the perspective of justice and, consequently, from the
perspective of others, a right is what can be demanded
vis-à-vis a debt. Because others owe it to me—although
this may mean respect or non-interference—I can
demand it. There is no exigency without indebtedness. One not insignificant consequence of this is
that, in order to be just, it is not necessary to wait for
the other to demand respect, restitution, compensation, etc. Justice does not wait for a demand; it gives

things when it must give them without waiting for the titular of the right to exercise his faculty to demand them.

## 4.  Variety of rights

Things are attributed to persons in very different ways. When it is said in the definition of justice that this virtue gives to each one *what is his own*, by "one's own" an attribution is generically intimated, thus encompassing every form of attribution. This follows the common usage, in which the possessive pronoun designates many forms of relation between a person and a thing or also between persons.

When someone speaks of his apartment, he does not necessarily mean to say that he is the owner; he can have the apartment as a rental. The same is not signified by the term "one's own" when it refers to one's name, objects or relatives.

And so, just as things are attributed to persons in very different ways, there are many kinds of rights. This is not the time to enumerate them. It is sufficient to note that things can be someone's rights in different respects.

## 5.  Title and measure of rights

The art of law has as its object *the declaration of rights* (*iuris dictio*), discerning the rights of persons and their extent. In other words, it has as its object the discernment of the *title* and *measure* of rights.

A title is that in which a right has its origin; or, said otherwise, it is that which causes the attribution of a thing to a specific subject. There are many classes of titles, but they can be reduced to human nature, legislation, custom, and agreements or contracts. For example, the title of the powers and functions of the Defender of the People in Spain is the Constitution of 1978. Many of our rights have their title in a contract: a contract of sale, a contract of transportation, rental, a loan, a contract for use, etc.

The first thing one must consider in order to figure out if something is a right is the title. And just as a right and *what is just* are the same thing—as we have repeatedly seen—in order to know when something is what is just, it is necessary to refer to the title. If there is no title, no matter how much one may say that "this is what is just," it is untrue; the expression "what is just" is used in an improper sense. We are well aware of the frequency with which it is said today that such and such a thing is what is just—and this has probably always happened. Since the jurist is the one who knows what is just and what is unjust, it is him who carefully separates *what is just* from *what is desirable* or the like. We already said earlier—the reader cannot claim to have misunderstood—that what is desirable, what makes a person happy, or what is fitting is not necessarily the same as what is just. It may be desirable that labourers make more money, but *what is just* is that they make what is indicated in the law, collective agreements or a labour contract. If the salary is an *inadequate salary*, it would certainly be unjust even if it is set by a law, contract or custom, because by natural title (by human nature) a salary must cover the vital necessities of the wage-earner and his family. Outside of this extreme case, though— which fortunately is scarcely found in countries like ours—*what is just* is that each person makes the stipulated amount. Some might say that a salary is unjust because such and such a rank deserves to have greater comparison with another; or they might use some other reason. (A salary would only be unjust, though, for the reason we gave above or something similar, such as disproportion between the amount of capital and the amount of work.) This is due to a confusion of what is just with what is desirable or with what are licit aspirations for a better life. If this is justice, then does it end up being clearly insufficient for a more human social life? On the one hand, justice alone (we have to repeat) makes society intolerable, but it is not legitimate to confuse these things. And the jurist knows this; and so, before invoking what is just, he asks for the title; and if there is no proof of a title, the jurist gives no attention to the matter.

In conjunction with the title, the jurist must recognise the measure of a right. No unlimited rights exist, nor are all rights equal. Property encompasses more faculties than the usufruct and the use. Legislation and contracts which grant rights can contain clauses which give them greater or lesser breadth. For example, Parliament does not have the same faculties in a presidential government as it does in a parliamentary government. According to different constitutions, the head of State can have more or fewer powers. In Spain, freedom to make a will is not the same in the common law established in the Civil Code for the country as it is in the diverse regional customary laws. And so on.

With title and measure, the jurist uncovers *what is just*: that which corresponds to the titular of the right, neither more nor less.

## 6.  Foundation of rights

Title is one thing, but the *foundation* of a right is something different. A title is that which attributes a thing to a subject as a right. On the other hand, the foundation is that in virtue of which a subject *can* be the subject of rights or of specific rights. For example, in order to be the King of Spain, according to article 57 of the current Constitution, it is necessary to be a successor according to the regular order of birthright and right of succession to His Majesty Don Juan Carlos I de Borbón. This condition of being a successor is the foundation for being king, but it is not the title; the title in the current law is the cited article of the Constitution.

The principal consequence of the differences between foundation and title is that the foundation enables one to be a titular of a right, but it does not grant a right; rights flow from a title. This point is worthy of consideration because there is no shortage of people who believe that they already have a right since they have the foundation.

Now that we have dealt with the foundation of rights, it is fitting to consider the ultimate foundation of every right—that is, what it is that enables a person to be *a subject of rights*. Why can a person possess rights, and, on the other hand, why do animals and stones not have rights? This question is elementary and, at the same time, among the most profound that can be asked with respect to rights. It is worthwhile to attempt a reply, especially because there are some in our time who speak of the rights of animals, which is something as acceptable in intention as it is absurd in expression.

Rights presuppose dominion over things. In one form or another, this means that things belong to the titular and therefore that they fall under his dominion. Moreover, though, the fact that things may be allotted and are simultaneously *due* implies not only true dominion but also that the titular of the things is not merely a part of the whole.

Let us consider the first aspect. It seems clear that, in order to be able to have dominion over one's environment, the first requirement is that one has dominion over his own being. It is conceivable that a being would have dominion over itself and not over its environment, but the contrary is inconceivable; for if one does not have dominion over himself, even less will he have dominion over other beings. This is the case with animals; there are animals that seem to have dominion over things in their environment, but such is not the case. Every animal is moved by means of forces and instincts over which it does not have mastery; more than dominating, it is dominated. Insofar as the animal is part of the movement of the cosmos, it is governed by the entirety of its forces. The animal does not belong to itself—it belongs to the universe; and for that matter nothing belongs to itself; nothing is properly its own. Among animals there are no thieves or assassins; what seems to belong to one is snatched away from it by another, and everything is but an interplay of all the forces which move the universe. Humans, on the other hand, have dominion over their own being; they are the master of themselves; this is the characteristic that constitutes them as *persons*. Humans are not moved exclusively by forces and biological instincts; ultimately, humans are responsible for their *personal acts*, because they freely decide by reason and will. Hence, they are capable of doing or not doing something, of choosing between distinct possibilities. They have dominion over their own being and are thus capable of having dominion over their environment. Therefore, they are capable of appropriating to themselves things which are due them. The foundation of the rights of human beings is the fact that they are persons.

One reaches the same conclusion by observing the second aspect indicated. Since things may be allotted in such a way that this attribution generates indebtedness, it is necessary that the titular not be simply part of the whole. A part, insofar as it is a part, has its reason for being in the fact that it is integrated into the whole. For example, humans see by means of their eyes; the eye does not have this function as a sphere of attribution autonomous from the person who sees. Hence, the eye has no reason to exist apart from the human body. As purely material beings, animals (and other beings) are mere parts of the universe. Their reason for being resides in the good of the cosmos, and this takes the form of being at the service of the whole. Hence, there are animals that are nourished by plants, and animals which are nourished by other animals; this is why there are animals and plants. Not being *distinct* from the universe or something other than parts of the universe, neither appropriation nor indebtedness is fitting, since a true *allotment* of things is not at stake. Everything is interconnected.

Humans are not pure matter; in virtue of their spiritual soul, which constitutes them as persons, they are not a mere part of the universe. For, in spiritual things, there cannot be a part of another being or a mixture. Since a spirit is *simple*, it does not have parts, nor can it be divided. For this reason it is said that a spirit is *incommunicable*—a word which here means that it cannot be considered *common in being* with other beings. The person opens him or herself to communion with others by knowledge and love but not by ontological integration (confusion in being). The result is that, since humans are not a mere part of a whole, they need there to be an *allotment* of the things of the universe;

they project themselves upon their environment also as an incommunicable being, and they therefore take possession of things as their own, not from the whole. With this we reach the same conclusion as before: rights are founded on the fact that humans are persons, that is, they are master of themselves.

From what we have just said, it can be observed that materialist positions do not sufficiently explain rights; and when materialism becomes radical—as happens with Marxism—rights are understood as superstructures which will necessarily disappear when humans part with their madness. At the same time, by obscuring the singularity of humans and the originality of their rights, materialism in the end attributes rights also to animals. It is clear that what is attributed to humans and animals is a faded version of rights more than real rights. Only in this way can it be minimally understood how the "rights" of sea lions and abortion, which is homicide, are defended at the same time.

# Chapter V

# Rights of Natural Law and Rights of Positive Law

## 1. Two kinds of laws

Several centuries before the Christian era, there were already traces of a traditional division of law: law is partly *natural* and partly *positive*. In reality, the adjective "positive" was not used until the Middle Ages, but other adjectives were employed earlier in its place, such as *legal* (what is proper to human legislation); such is the case with Aristotle, who distinguished between what is naturally just and what is legally just. Roman jurists used a twofold division (the law of the nations or natural law, and civil law) or a threefold division (natural law, the law of the nations, and civil law). Beginning in the 19th century, *juridical positivism* expanded itself, mixed with theories according to which only positive law would be properly considered law. Natural law, rather than law, would be morals, relative values, logical structures, the nature of things, etc., or it would simply not exist. This is not the appropriate place to enter into a subject which goes beyond an elementary book like this one; it is sufficient for us to produce evidence that the phenomenon of positivism exists.

## 2. Positive rights

By positive rights [*derecho*] we mean every right whose title and measure owes its origin to the human will, whether it be a piece of legislation, a custom, or a contract. It is not necessary to repeat that we are speaking of rights in their proper sense—the just thing, one's own—not of legislation or norms in general.

What is meant by the existence of positive rights? It means that there are things allotted by humans themselves or, said otherwise, that there are things whose attribution is an act of the human will. This is a common experience. When a municipal government marks some streets as one-way and others as two-way in order to direct traffic, it posts signs, it marks crosswalks, etc.; among different possible uses, the use of the surface of streets in a city is allotted; it assigns and regulates spaces and times for those who travel about the city with or without a car. It is regulating rights. To travel about on the right side (or on the left in Great Britain) is the driver's right vis-à-vis those who drive in the opposite direction, as is it the pedestrian's right to travel about preferably on a crosswalk marked by lines, etc.

We have experienced another example in the preparation of the Constitution. Using means of communication, we could be present at the debates regarding the powers and functions which should be assigned to the principal organs of the State and, earlier, which these organs should be. There was discussion about the separation of governance powers and functions and their titular, just as there was discussion about the distribution of functions between the State and autonomous communities. Once a consensus was reached and, in every case, after the prescribed votes were made, the prevalent opinion was established as a draft, which ultimately would have juridical force after coming into effect as the Constitution.

This same phenomenon is found in relationships among individuals. All commerce supposes a redistribution of a product sold and the money paid, which causes a change in the titular. There is an allotment with each will, each work contract, etc. Human relationships undergo an uninterrupted transfer of things, which supposes a continuous redistribution of goods. Rights which take their origin in and are modified by such human activity are *positive rights*.

## 3.  Limits of positive rights

Positive means *posited*, not given to humans without having been established (posited) by them. In this regard, it is fitting to ask about limitations on this capacity of humans. Is the capacity of human beings to establish and regulate rights unlimited? Does it include the whole sphere of human social life? If not, what is the criterion which sets limits?

When the British wish to demonstrate the powers enjoyed by their country's Parliament in a graphic manner, they are accustomed to say that their Parliament can do *everything* with the exception of making a man a woman and a woman a man; that is to say, it can do everything that it is possible for humans to do. Even though the British do not say it, it is evident that there are other things that their Parliament cannot do, beyond making a man a woman.

The saying is humorous, and it is necessary to interpret it in this light. It does not refer to the physical fact of transforming a man into a woman. The British would not say this of their Parliament, even in jest—though perhaps they would say it about their physicians. What this little expression means is that the British Parliament does not have the ability to issue a bill in virtue of which a man is socially treated like a woman and vice-versa. The Parliament does not have the power to create so great an absurdity. We would do well to inquire, though: would such a law be an absurdity or would it also be an injustice? There is no doubt that this absurdity would be an injustice.

Hence, we are all substantially convinced of this: humans cannot be treated how others or how titulars of power may wish or desire, since there are things which are unjust by their very nature. In other words, there are things which *are not indifferent* with respect to justice. Whether cars travel on the right side or the left side, *provided that they travel on one side or the other*, of itself makes no difference. The English can think that traveling on the right side is stubbornness on the part of the rest of the world; and the rest of the world has the complete right to think that traveling on the left side is an extravagance of the English. Both are worthy opinions, because it is certain that traveling on one side or the other in itself is neither good nor bad, neither just nor unjust: it is a free choice. It is not a free choice, though, for two trains to travel about without limitations or deviations by the same route and in the opposite direction. For they will either be halted at the place where they meet, and then the right of the passengers (which includes reaching their destination) will be injured; or they will be halted by the force of the collision, in which case the passengers' right to life and physical integrity will be injured. Four centuries before our era, Aristotle observed that there are things in the law which are inherently indifferent and there are things which are not indifferent.

Humans *can* (meaning, according to justice) create and regulate rights in the sphere of what is indifferent. What does indifferent mean? It does not mean that a choice is not better or worse than another from the technical point of view; it can be that a technical study demonstrates that traveling on the right or left side is technically better than the opposite. Indifferent ultimately means that, with respect to justice and morality, adopting one solution or the other is the same, since neither harms justice or any other sphere of morality. Whether the Scottish wear kilts could be more or less disagreeable, but it is indifferent; stealing money is not indifferent.

In this respect, it is fitting that one knows how to distinguish, on the one hand, what is just and what is unjust, what is morally correct or morally incorrect, and, on the other hand, what is a standard of socially acceptable behaviour. In one environment, a type of activity can be marginal or socially unacceptable; this usually gives rise to an awareness of good or bad activity, which must be clearly distinguished from an awareness of what is just and what is unjust (an awareness of good and bad morals). The sociological standard of action leads to an identification of what is sociologically *normal or abnormal*; and consequently, a person either makes a *judgement that it is suitable* to adapt him or herself to what is normal, or he or she reacts with non-conformism. On the other hand, identifying what is just or unjust (what is good or evil in the moral sense) leads to an awareness that one is conforming or not conforming with what human nature demands. In other words, standards of socially acceptable behaviour pertain to the field of *what is indifferent*. Contrariwise, what concerns justice is never indifferent.

Therefore, the field of positive law is clearly limited: its possible subject matter is *that which is indifferent*. Hence, in order to distinguish whether a norm is of positive law or natural law, it is necessary to consider its degree of indifference with respect to human nature. To the extent that it is indifferent, it will tend to be of positive law.

We said that the *possible* subject matter of positive law is what is indifferent. I refer to *possibility* because the subject matter is indifferent until it is established as a right by an act of human will. Once it becomes a right it is no longer indifferent but it is what is just for the titular. For instance, it is indifferent that a certain portion of land destined for colonisation is assigned to this or that settler; there is nothing requiring that this parcel must by nature be occupied by such and such a person. Once it is assigned, though, it becomes attributed to its titular, and it is no longer indifferent that another settler invades this parcel and takes possession of it: this would be unjust.

## 4.  Natural rights

We have just seen in brief strokes what positive rights are; let us now consider what natural rights are. By the term "natural rights" we understand every right whose title is not the human will but human nature and whose measure is the nature of humans or the nature of things.

A moment ago, I said that the potential subject matter of positive law is *what is indifferent*. In order to explain this we also saw that there are things which are not indifferent with respect to justice. In the order of justice, it is not logical to think or say that respecting the life of an innocent person or killing him or her are the same thing, that it is indifferent to defraud one's neighbour or to be honest, or that raising and educating children is the same thing as leaving them in the street or mistreating them. Certain modern mentalities and ideologies seemingly attempt to defy common sense about these things.

I ask the reader to make an effort to forget these approaches and ideological manipulations and to try to be reasonable. Can someone *seriously and in his heart of hearts* think that it is indifferent, that it is therefore not unjust, or that it is only a relative *value* for parents to kill their children and cast them into the garbage can so that they may be able to take quiet vacations? Let us not be too hasty by using logic: what would be implied in affirming that this or other similar conduct that is more or less serious violates only a *relative value* (as relativism says) or a standard of socially acceptable behaviour (as sociology affirms)? By definition, a relative value is something which is good or valuable not in and of itself but only because a person or a group of persons give it value or esteem it. A social standard of behaviour is a norm of conduct, in itself indifferent, but accepted by the consensus of the majority. Maintaining that the conduct cited above only violates a relative value or a merely social norm would imply (by definition) that such conduct is not in itself evil or unjust but only that others or the majority *perceive it or appraise it* as evil. One who does such a thing is not truly doing evil; rather he carries out something that in itself is neither good nor evil. The logical conclusion follows with total, thorough clarity: *offenders do not commit anything that is evil in itself*; rather they do things that others *opine* to be evil. In other words, if they are punished with penalties, the punishment is not merited in the proper sense; it only represents the violent reaction of the majority. In reality, offenders are marginalised in society without any fault other than performing conduct which the majority *does not look upon favourably*. If the reader thinks that one who murders, assaults, injures, slanders, beats others, etc., is more than a person who behaves in a manner that differs from the majority, it is evident that he takes account of the fact that there are things that are inherently just and things that are inherently unjust. Well then, this is the key point of natural law.

Earlier I asked the reader to try to be reasonable. In effect, saying that there are inherently just things and inherently unjust things means (going back to Greek Antiquity) that there are things which conform to the natural postulates of right reason (conforming with natural reason) and that there are postulates which are contrary to right reason. And so it is said that what natural reason dictates as just or unjust is from natural law or is contrary to it. So said the Stoics several centuries before Jesus Christ, and so it continues to be said up to the present day. Natural law proclaims nothing other than this: that, in specific areas of human activity, there is rational behaviour and irrational behaviour; there is behaviour that is in accord with right reason and behaviour that is contrary to it.

Now then, since the proper act of reason is to know, if it grasps things as being inherently just or unjust, evidently this is because it knows something objective, with realism and consistency. This is the *objective criterion of what is just and what is unjust*, in virtue of which there is behaviour which respects or injures goods that are not indifferent. This objective thing is the human person inasmuch as he or she represents an individuation of human nature. In other words, what reason grasps is that the human person is a *titular of rights* and that his or her nature is the foundation and criterion of these rights. We have already said that if subjective awareness is what grasps the notions of what is just and unjust, everything would be reduced to a contest of opinions; as we have seen, this is unreasonable. Hence, it is reason and not subjective awareness which knows that what is just and what is unjust is not indifferent. This is the system of natural law (not a specific precept of natural law, which we have not yet spoken about).

A natural right is that which is just in itself, that which is not indifferent. And how is it that just things exist by nature, that is, a naturally just thing, a natural right? If we recall the notion of rights which we have given, to speak of the existence of what is naturally just means that there are things (goods, powers, faculties, etc.) *attributed to persons* not by an agreement or a consensus among humans but in virtue of what is *natural* to humans—that is, factors and dimensions proper to their being. The reader might question this: do such things exist in the person him or herself? What would you say, reader, if, while walking quietly down the street, an ambulance stops on the roadside and, without any explanation, physicians descend upon and seize you, removing your cornea in order to give sight to a blind person or to conduct an experiment? Would you not feel that you were treated unjustly? Would you find comfort if they told you that this feeling of being an object of injustice is nothing more than your own opinion—just as respectable as a contrary opinion—and therefore that they actually committed nothing unjust against you?

Since I do not know the reader, I do not know how he will reply to these questions, but I presume that he will say that he is the master of his eyes and that no one can deprive him of them without his consent. This is what we as humans are used to saying, and, what is more important, it is what is deduced from the notion of the person. Earlier we said that the person is a being that is the master of himself. He is therefore not only *capable* of having dominion over his environment, but by nature he is already the master and owner of himself. At the very least, everything which constitutes human beings *is attributed to them* in virtue of the fact that they are persons. Hence, it is evident that humans have natural rights. If students of law are taught that a right is what is due, they will learn that humans have other natural rights beyond the goods which constitute their being and their natural ends (life, physical integrity, free manifestation of their thoughts, religion or religious freedom, health, etc.). Now is not the time to speak of these, though; it has simply been necessary to present evidence of the fact that natural rights exist, and this is what we just did.

Since natural law has human nature as its foundation and title, *it is not indifferent*; and since all human beings are *equally* persons and the nature of everyone is the same, natural law is the same among all humans and in all places—as Aristotle once observed.

I realise that those who question the relevance of natural law for philosophy and for the science of law are not thinkers of little import. Everything that concerns the human person raises many and very profound problems, but this is an introduction, not a treatise.

## 5.  Natural measure of rights

As we were just saying, natural rights refer to the title of rights, not their measure. Let us say a few words, then, about the latter.

There is no doubt that there are natural measures of rights. If natural rights have human nature as their title, then human nature is also the criterion for their extension and their limitations. Moreover, though, we all have experience of the fact that there are rights whose measure is natural. As the reader will recall, my friend to whom I freely loaned five dollars (that is, with the obligation of returning the same quantity of money to me without interest) must return precisely five dollars to me. Why? No one wonders if five dollars is a quantity equal to five dollars, for this is evident to the majority of people: both quantities are equal by the nature of things (is mathematics even needed here?). Here we have an example of a natural measure, not a conventional or indifferent one. There are many other examples which anyone can discover with little effort.

It will be observed that, with respect to measure—not referring to title—we have used two expressions: the nature of the human person and the nature of things. Without confusing them, both can be a measure of rights as the situation warrants, but the first refers to the being and ends of the person, while the second encompasses the being, qualities, quantities, etc. *of things.*

## 6.  Mixed rights

As frequently happens in this life whenever there is advancement in the knowledge of something (above all in the sciences), more questions always arise and everything becomes more complex. On this occasion, though, we leave the complications aside for books that are more substantial than a simple introduction like this.

For now I am going to limit myself to complicat-
ing the reader's life only a little. In addition to *purely*
natural and positive rights (those whose title and
measure are natural or positive) there are mixed
rights; that is, there may be rights which have a natural title and a concrete measure that is positive, and
vice-versa. Let us propose some examples. We are
free by nature; the right to travel throughout the
whole world is a natural right, but human laws can
regulate this right by placing limits on it. They can
demand from us a duly-issued passport or visa in
order to enter a country; they can demand certifica-
tion that we have been vaccinated or that we are not
infected with a contagious disease, etc. A right with a
natural title can have the measure of a positive right.

The inverse also happens; the example given
earlier is useful. To lend a quantity of money is a
contract, and the rights and obligations that arise
from it are positive; but if the loan is gratuitous, the
measure of the quantity to be returned is determined
by a natural measure.

Is this relevant for the jurist? It very much is,
since those who are not jurists frequently confuse
things, seeing injustices where there are none or, the
reverse, accepting things as just which are not. As an
example, let us analyse the oft-posed and treated
problem of being on a pension. It is reasonably said
that pensions are many times too small; they are
*unjust*. What is the just thing with respect to pensions? The jurist, who must be the first one to ask
this, should distinguish the natural and positive

elements of pensions. Are pensions a natural right? It is a natural right that one who has worked in a normal manner in life and who reaches a time in which he must retire from work receives what is suitable in order to live. This is what is natural. Pensions are a positive form of fulfilling a natural *obligation*; therefore, indebtedness is natural with respect to its origin, but it is positive with respect to the form in which it is paid. This has an important consequence. Natural law does not determine the measure of the right to collect a pension (the exact quantity of money to receive); but positive law does. That is, it is the State that determines what quantity of its recourses is destined for pensions and how the money is divided among the distinct retirees. The result is that what is just (what a retiree must collect) is determined by positive law. The retiree has a *right* to this quantity and nothing more. What then happens if these quantities are insufficient? It then happens that if the retiree, after making an agreement with some Social Security civil servant, should have an administrative irregularity on his hands and collects more than what was indicated (but not going beyond what is sufficient to live), the civil servant and the retiree would commit fraud—a true injustice against the State.

What about the fact that the retiree ought to receive a suitable living? There is agreement that, since this obligation *does not primarily fall upon the State but on society*, the latter has the obligation to provide what the State cannot; for example, those close to the retiree must come to his aid. If it is nevertheless maintained that it is more fitting for Social Security to be responsible for the whole burden, it must not be forgotten that there is a form prescribed by the natural law for fulfilling this obligation; therefore, the solution of burdening Social Security with it is one *legitimate aspiration*, not a right in the strict sense. Therefore, the way to transform this aspiration into a right is characteristic of legitimate aspirations: political measures, that is, petitions, demonstrations, press campaigns, etc.

We say that many pensions in our country are currently insufficient. This is certain, but the conclusion based on everything we have said is that the injustice does not fall only upon the State but also upon society and upon family members. Each person must bear his portion of an injustice.

## 7.  Connection between natural rights and positive rights

The relationship between natural rights and positive rights is a central point of the science of law. Limiting oneself only to positive rights necessarily leads to injustice, and the jurist is entrusted with the center of the road in exercising his art and his craft.

Since this matter is very important—so much so that if it were not taught to a student in his faculty, he should study it on his own—we are not going to deal with it in this introduction, which does not attempt to teach one to be a jurist (this would be a useless pretension) but to describe the general components of the profession.

Nevertheless, I cannot resist giving some attention to an urgent matter which, in my judgement, concerns the knowledge of jurists. The positivistic mentality extending into certain areas has created among some (positivists or not) the habit of perceiving positive law in a more natural manner without its indispensable reference to natural law. It seems normal to them to speak of and apply positive law without a close connection to natural law, without taking account of the fact that positive law is inexplicable without natural law. Why is it inexplicable? For then, without natural law positive law does not have the necessary presupposition of exigency.

It is within everyone's reach to understand that a cultural fact that does not have a natural basis is impossible. Everything that humans make or invent requires natural capacity; this is what philosophers call *potency*. In order to see, a person must have eyes. On the basis of this natural fact, someone can construct a series of cultural works: writing, painting, sculpture, television, cinema, etc. If humans did not have vision, however, all these cultural works would not exist. Humans are incapable of flying by themselves; try as they might, they will never extend any wings (the body is incapable of having them). However, on the basis of a series of natural data (the weight and resistance of materials, laws of aerodynamics, etc.), they can construct some apparatus

with which to fly (from delta wings to the most complicated jet plane). It is axiomatic that *every cultural
work depends on natural data*. This is why it is said that
humans *invent* (a word which means "finding," to
discover something that already was, at least in
potency) and not that they *create* (to make something
out of nothing). Humans are inventors, not creators.

Given the axiom stated, pretending that only
positive law exists, that is, that every law is posited
by humans, contradicts the most elementary common sense; for if there is something that is culturally
juridical (positive), it necessarily has to find its
beginning in something naturally juridical. It is
rightly observed that the axiom does not mean that
a cultural work is possible with respect to any
potency or capacity, but specifically that humans
have a potency of the same order as the cultural
work; for example, hearing is not sufficient for the
realisation of cultural works related to vision. It is
therefore axiomatic that, if a positive (cultural) juridical work exists, it has to be fixed in a natural juridicity. If there were nothing naturally juridical, there
would be nothing culturally juridical. Hence, the
best demonstration that natural law exists is the fact
that positive law exists.

What is the minimum, natural juridicity that
must exist in order for a positive right to exist? If we
recall that a right is one's own thing, it becomes evident that the minimum, natural juridicity which
must exist is the condition of being a subject of the
rights proper to humans. Here is something that

cannot possibly proceed from positive law. The condition of being a subject of rights is the *natural potency* necessary for humans to be able to be attributed rights or to attribute rights to others. To say that a human law gives the condition of being a subject of rights is an affirmation emptied by its own radical impossibility: humans would be giving themselves potency (capacity for a cultural work) and the act (the cultural work), which would suppose in them the power of a creator in the strict sense (to make something out of nothing); such a thing is impossible.

If positive rights exist, it is evident that humans are naturally subjects of rights. And what in their beings makes them subjects of rights? We were discussing this in the pages above: in order for humans to possess something as their own, they must be in possession of their own beings, that is, they must be persons. Therefore, by being persons humans are titulars of natural rights. It is well observed that the capacity to be a titular of positive rights is not a mere potency (capacity); but it arises from being a titular of natural rights. This should not be surprising since every positive right is built upon some natural right.

This is the unavoidable *aporia of positivism*: if natural rights do not exist, it is impossible for positive rights to exist; and if positive rights exist, natural rights necessarily exist.

# Chapter VI

# Legislation

## 1. Knowledge of legislation

We have already seen that the jurist (a man of law) is also customarily called a *man/woman of laws* (or legislation). Although legislation must not be confused with the law, it is not therefore necessary to reject this title; on the contrary, understanding legislation—knowing legislation—forms a very important part of the task of the jurist.

Knowing legislation—that is, understanding and interpreting it correctly—is an art, which is not within everyone's reach. It is very easy to fall into the caricaturised figure of the *petty lawyer*—he who does not go beyond the letter of the law—the counterfeit of the man of laws, who must be a jurist. I do not know if the reader will recall a film called *La loi, c'est la loi*, starring Fernandel and Totó; its humour is based on the bizarre situations that arise when the law is followed literally. The reader will recall what the Bible says when speaking of the law: the letter kills.

The difficulty of interpreting law is not due to the use of rare or little-known terms; the majority of statutes are written in a form that is accessible to persons of common culture, and in every case it is not very difficult to familiarise oneself with the language. Except when they treat highly specialised matters, laws are usually written in rather common language. Our Constitution can be read; scarcely will one find a word in it whose meaning requires consultation of a dictionary or encyclopaedia.

The difficulty lies in the fact that the interpretation of laws demands a particular *prudence*, a special expression of that virtue called prudence of the law; in Latin, this is *iuris prudentia*, from which comes the English word *jurisprudence*.[4] Just as language has the Royal Academy of Language, so the science of law has a royal academy in Spain: the *Royal Academy of Jurisprudence*, which is the classical name for the science of law. (The complete name is the *Royal Academy of Jurisprudence and Legislation*.)

At the present time, the word jurisprudence is commonly reserved for designating the juridical doctrine which comes from the sentences of a Supreme Tribunal and, more generally, from the decisions of other tribunals. Knowing how to interpret the law is sometimes called the juridical science or the science of law. This is so for two reasons. First, some hold the opinion that, more than being a virtue,

---

4. Translator's note: Of course, here the author refers not to the English but to the Spanish word *jurisprudencia*.

applying the law is a technique, the juridical technique. The other reason is due to the fact that, with the appearance of juridical dogmatism, there was an attempt to make law a speculative science.

Fortunately, the second reason is scarcely found today. After the excesses of juridical dogmatism and conceptualism, and also once the fairly proximate attempts to reduce juridical reasoning to mathematical formulae were frustrated, the practicality of juridical knowledge once more began to regain its place. Nor does the first reason have sufficient weight since it stands in relation to the second. Technique evokes the *practical application* of speculative knowledge, such that *juridical technique* would be the application of concepts and speculatively construed dogmas to the concrete case by the *science of law* (a speculative science according to this opinion). Well, since the science of law is an essentially practical knowledge, although it may also be composed of speculative perceptions, it must consist of a *habit*—an ability or aptitude—of practical reason by which one can come to know (in each case) which rights are at stake and how legislation must be interpreted. It happens, though, that the intellectual habit of *knowing how to act correctly* is called the virtue of prudence. The science of law (a practical one) is a kind of prudence. Therefore, the Royal Academy has every right to continue referring to itself as "of *Jurisprudence*"; the true name of the science of law (a practical science) is *jurisprudence*, just like the Roman jurists referred to it.

Perhaps some find all of this annoying, thinking that, in the end, the law is the law; and where it
says "wax," there is no more wax than what burns.
These are only the complications of petty lawyers,
since bread means bread, and wine means wine.
Indeed, this is certain; but we recall how many
kinds, qualities and varieties of bread and wine
there are; and perhaps one imperfectly sees that
where it says wine, it is necessary to have the careful
skill of knowing which wine it is fitting to serve; it
may not be fitting to serve to friends a more common wine on a wedding day or a very fine burgundy
on a normal day at a typical meal. *Fittingness* and
*careful skill in judging* are part of prudence.

The student of law does not first and foremost
attend a faculty in order to learn the text of laws; he
goes to acquire a *juridical mentality*, that is, the habit
of jurisprudence, the prudence of the law. To this
end, it will be necessary to take in hand as essential
material the Constitution, the Civil, Penal and Com-
mercial Codes, the Laws of Civil and Criminal Judicial Process, and other legislative texts.[5] Nevertheless,
this does not mean that memorisation of these is
required; one will need to study these laws, but
the examinations will be based instead on the manuals and the explanations from class, since what is

---

5. Translator's note: The author writes in a codified legal system. In
   Anglo-American legal systems Federal, Provincial or State revised
   statutes, and other compilations of statutes could have been mentioned as examples.

important above all is that one knows the *interpretation* of the laws. One will always have the text of the laws in hand; and one may wish to have cheap and manageable versions of them. It is good for one to be clear about this; let there not be a repetition of the event which happened to one student many years ago (when the Civil Code cost 10 quarters, 2,50 *pesetas*[6]) who apparently had not been advised of how things went. At that time there was a professor of civil law from the University of Barcelona, Prof. Joaquín Dualde, a well-known and innovative civil jurist. After examining the student mentioned, he always gave him a most disappointing failing mark. The student protested, alleging that he knew the whole Civil Code from memory. This is a feat that is by no means easy, achieved only by unique memories with arduous effort. The professor was unmoved, though; after showing himself steady, he challenged him in a manner both serious and humorous: "Then you have a 25-cent knowledge of the civil law." This strengthens our position; knowing the law by memory does not make one a jurist, just as knowing the Bible by memory does not make one a master of Biblical exegesis. By this I do not mean that the student of law would not do well to commit some articles of the law to memory; this always makes a good impression in oral examinations, and in certain arguments it can be the key to success.

---

6. Translator's note: This amount in former Spanish currency is the equivalent of about C$0.25.

## 2. Legislation

That which is customarily called a law, a statute, an act [*ley*] in common language is called *a norm* in more specialised language. The use of the latter word is quite modern, although it was introduced as a result of the principle of the *hierarchy of norms*. According to this principle, not all norms have the same value. Some are more valuable than others in the sense that if those on a lower level contradict those on a higher level, they are considered either null or annullable, depending on the case and distinct juridical systems. This principle is relatively modern, although any norm contrary to an earlier one derogated from it or abrogated it (a partial derogation); or they would both simply continue to be valid, and in this case jurists would understand them by attempting to reconcile them. All of them were generically called laws [*leyes*], but they would receive distinct names according to the form of the document in which they were written or according to the form of their wording: royal decree, statutes, etc. Beginning with the introduction of the hierarchy of norms, the name reflects a greater or lesser ranking: a constitution (or constitutional law), law (or ordinary law), decree-law, decree, a ministerial order, etc. This whole collection receives the name of *norms* and, in current usage, laws [*leyes*]. Here, for the sake of convenience, we will speak without the distinctions of law or norms.

A law is an obligatory rule which has a *general* character. By *general* we do not mean that it refers to all citizens but that it is destined for a more or less broad collectivity of persons—in contrast with *precepts* or *orders* which are directed individually to a person or determined, unified group. For instance, the general rules of organisation or conduct for soldiers are laws or norms (from royal statutes to governmental decrees); on the other hand, the mandates that entrust a sergeant to a soldier or a captain to a company are orders or precepts. This all becomes complicated, though, since, by application of the principle of the hierarchy of norms, there are precepts which are given *in the form of law* or *decrees* or other forms. If this satisfies the reader, though, we are going to leave aside these complications and restrict ourselves to the concept of law as an obligatory rule of conduct with a general character.

## 3.  Social norm

A law governs and orders relationships among people; it is thus a social rule or a norm in the life of society. In order to understand its nature, it is necessary to take two things into account. In the first place, that it is an obligatory rule, carrying an obligation in the proper sense. What is meant by *obligation in the proper sense*? It means that it does not simply concern a rule of conduct whose non-observance produces social rejection. Here we encounter sociological standards of behaviour which must be clearly distinguished from laws.

We humans frequently impose determined norms of behaviour which we say one is *obliged* to follow, though they are not laws. For example, even still—or at least so it was up to recent times—in some hotels one is *obliged* to wear a necktie in order to enter and remain in its parlours; even if one is an important person, lacking a necktie he is invited (and if the case requires it, obliged) to leave the hotel parlours. To be sure, this is not particular only to refined ambiences; someone might try to wear a necktie and other fine clothing in less favourable ambiences, and it will probably take him less time to be expelled than if one goes without a tie to one of the hotels mentioned earlier. One is *obliged* to go into some ambiences all dressed up, while one is *obliged* to go into others with shabby dress. Are these true obligations in the proper sense? The response is negative. Breaking a simple social behavioural norm is only a matter of non-conformity, lack of concern or, in an extreme case, a desire to annoy one's neighbours or provoke them. Outside of ill intentions, though, the non-fulfillment of this norm does not suppose a violation of any value that is essential to the human person. One can be an upright and faultless person with or without a necktie, and he or she can be a scoundrel clothed in a dress coat or in cowboy pants. With respect to personal values, we are in the area of what is *indifferent*.

If we at times do not clearly see the difference between an obligation in the proper sense and these *improper obligations*, it is due to a lack of education. Parents and teachers on occasion have the bad practice of correcting the slapping of a companion in the face and eating with one's hands with the same tone and the same anger. In this regard, I recall the tact and instructive ability of one father. This father was hearing Mass with one of his children, and as the moment of Communion approached, he asked the little child if he was going to receive Communion. The child replied that he could not do so without going to Confession, since he had exchanged a fountain pen which his grandparents had just given him for some trinket; this was an action which he did in bad conscience. To the boy's great relief, the father replied, "Do not worry, my son; this is not a sin; it is bad business."

In social life, it is necessary not to confuse a *sin* (a crime or an injustice) with *bad business*, that is, with a lack of education, non-conformity to social habits, folly or unusual behaviour—all of which provoke social rejection (which can be *bad business*). The first refers to obligations in the proper sense; the second concerns improper obligations. The first is *an obligation* properly speaking, and the second is the *agreeability* of acting in conformity with a commonly accepted standard of behaviour in a social context. Non-fulfillment of *an obligation* is immoral, which can constitute an injustice since it is behaviour that does not correspond with the condition of the person. Non-fulfillment of what are called *social obligations* is to expose oneself to social rejection, and, to this extent, it is fitting and opportune to fulfill them; but in any case, their non-fulfillment does not damage anything fundamental to the human person insofar as there can be an error but not an immorality or injustice. What is more, sometimes fulfilling *social obligations* can constitute an *obligation* of conscience.

Obeying the law pertains to *obligation*. It is not simply fitting, although we on occasion comply with laws moved by motives of fittingness—for example, to avoid a fine. Laws mark what we *in justice* owe to society. Society has some obligations with respect to us as citizens: this is what is called *distributive justice*. In forming part of society, we as persons have the strict right to the enjoyment of social goods by all according to just criteria and legitimately established rules (this is strict justice). The goods of society must be *distributed* among all citizens with respect to their use and according to other modalities. And the truth is that we tend to be zealous about this right. How many complaints there are! There is scarcely a conversation in which the State or society is not criticised in one way or another for what we consider to be a deficient or unjust distribution of goods. Our zeal for this justice makes us on-edge.

Nevertheless, we are inclined to forget that we as citizens also have obligations of justice with respect to society and the State. Society has the right to have us as citizens assume our obligations of justice toward society, to have us respect society's rights vis-à-vis its citizens. This type or kind of justice is *legal justice*. And so there are not only the obligations of justice among individuals (justice which receives the name *commutative justice*) or those of society with respect to its citizens (*distributive justice*); there are also citizens' obligations of justice toward society (*legal justice*).

Even though we are used to being equally on-edge about obligations of legal justice, our concerns are the opposite than what they are with respect to distributive justice. We seek out the greatest number of excuses for feeling free of such obligations, and we argue about how many rights society and the State have. It is a form of weak love for justice. Hence, the person who has a true love of justice, the integrally just person, is detected by his compliance with legal justice. Moreover, when we admire a person as just—he or she is a *just person*, we say—even if we are unaware of it, we fix our attention on everything he or she does to fulfill legal justice without stinginess and with generosity.

Our obligations to society are of a different nature: some pertain to justice, some to other virtues (e.g., solidarity). Which are the obligations of justice? Which are those which represent *the just thing* (neither more nor less) which we owe to society and the State? What we owe to society, as something proper to society, depends on our collaboration and participation. Society is nothing other than a unity of all of us with respect to the ends and goods which are obtained by the effort of us all (the common purpose or the common good). That which belongs to society—that is, not what is the property of society but what *is proper to it*—that which it must obtain, and that for which it exists is the common purpose or common good. Now then, just as society is a union of all, what each one owes to society is his *quota of participation* in the attainment of the common good (this is our term). The portion which each one must contribute in order for society to obtain the common good is the *right* of society and each citizen's *obligation of justice*.

It is fitting, though, that we ask ourselves: what marks this quota? What establishes this obligation of distributing the common effort among all? Logically, it will be that which governs and orders the conduct of all the citizens with respect to the common good. Indeed, such a function is proper to laws. They are what mark the obligation of each citizen to govern and order social life. The law marks the obligations of legal justice. At this point, I am supposing that one will have already guessed the reasoning for calling this justice *legal*: because it consists of complying with laws.

Obeying laws then is an obligation of justice; it is an *obligation*, not something that it is fitting to do in order to avoid social rejection. The obligatory nature of laws is based on justice. Since we are members of society and since we are obliged to fulfill our responsibility for obtaining the common good, we are obliged to comply with what is mandated by the law, which is the *rule of justice* for citizens with respect to society.

## 4. Legislation and moral obligation

We were saying earlier that it would be necessary to take into account two things in order to understand the nature of law. We have seen one: a law is an *obligation*; it does not pertain to some social practices or simply social standards of behaviour. Now we have to consider the second. Humans have obligations which are not imposed by laws. We are all aware that *moral obligations* exist: to love God and neighbour, to speak the truth, to be chaste, not to slander, etc.

*a)* Among these moral obligations some will never be included in laws since they do not fall within its competence. There is a portion of our activity which is outside the jurisdiction of the laws of society; this includes our private life and our self-determination. It would be an abuse for laws to attempt to enter into these matters. When the State usurps the function of entering into that which pertains to our private life and the sphere of our self-determination, it becomes *totalitarian*. There are *totalitarianisms* of the left and there are those of the right; either way, the same is true: they can all be rejected as contrary to human freedom.

Self-determination in these spheres is free, but freedom refers to the fact that laws do not have jurisdiction, not to the absence of obligations. In our conscience we know that we have obligations and grave obligations: they are the moral obligations which are summed up in the Ten Commandments of the Law of God.

These obligations represent demands of our nature and of our condition as men and women. By being persons, our being is *dignified*; we cannot act according to our appetites, nor can others treat us capriciously. This is the grandeur of the human being. By being endowed with spirit and reason, he must conduct himself in accord with his being, in conformity with that which is and with natural ends. This is the obligation of authenticity, of conducting oneself according to what one is. If humans do not act *rationally*—according to natural law, that is, in accord with the ends to which one is destined by nature—if they do not live authenticity (which does not consist of making oneself his own law, but of living in conformity with what one objectively is), he is *degraded*, and he offends himself by offending his own dignity. This is the content of immorality.

In its more profound basis, a moral obligation is the law of God. Humans have been created by God, man and woman, insofar as his or her being represents a divine gift and his or her natural ends constitute divine blessing, the good which he or she has been called to fully actualise. A moral obligation is an obligation before God; and contravening it, as well as offending human dignity, violates the law of God and constitutes an offense against Him. This offense against God is what turns immorality into *a sin*.

Now then, all of this is studied not by the *jurist* but by the *moralist* (a philosopher or a theologian); and judging sin does not belong to tribunals but to the Church, particularly the confessor. When we sin, in order to re-establish peace in our conscience, we have recourse not to a court but to the sacrament of Confession.

*b)* In addition to the spheres of our private life and self-determination about which we have spoken, we encounter other spheres in which laws coincide with morality. Theft is a sin, and at the same time it is a crime; such an action is judged in Confession and in court. Does this mean that in these cases the jurist is a moralist; are *morality* and *law* the same thing? There is a juridical rule that is very easy to understand: *non bis in idem*; there is no judging the same thing twice. If a person has committed a crime, he is judged, the corresponding penalty is imposed, and the matter is finished. It would not be logical to judge him a second time the following month and then another time and so on as many times as one may wish. Once a matter is judged, the appropriate recourses are granted to the interested parties; and once the recourses are exhausted, it is said that the matter passes into the state of an adjudged matter, and there is no returning to it. Well then, to continue the example used, for the one who commits a crime, being at peace with one's conscience (ultimately with God) is not the same as being at peace with society. Cleansing a sin committed by one's action is not the same as cleansing the crime against society implied by this action. The same action has a twofold aspect and a twofold judgement: the judgement of conscience (in this case, the judgement of the confessor) and the judgement before the tribunal. We have all seen in films the example of a delinquent who, after a life of crime, is seized by the police, judged, and sentenced to prison. When he leaves prison, the individual in question *withdraws himself* from the crime and establishes a legal practice or dedicates himself to rest after declaring that *he is at peace with society*. It is true; he is at peace with society since he will not again be detained, nor will the judgement be rescinded. However, is he at peace with his conscience; is he at peace with God? Certainly not; such peace is only regained by sincere conversion of the heart, by repentance. *To sin* is not the same as *to be guilty*.

What does all this tells us? It tells us something very important. Even if laws and morality coincide in a specific matter, the jurist is not a moralist, because the *juridical aspect* and the *moral aspect* of an action are distinct. The reality, the action (the behaviour) is one, but the perspectives from which it is seen by the jurist and by the moralist do not coincide. At the same time, the laws which govern society (those which correspond to the jurist) refer to human behaviour in a determined aspect: that of the person's participation in the common good or the general interest. Humans as citizens are concerned with laws, and within society they exhaust their regulated action. Law is directed to making a person a good citizen: the interior realm of the heart pertains to the person and to God. Laws are *rules of justice*; as we have seen, their specific obligatory nature—which belongs to them as rules of conduct owed to society—is based on the obligation of justice to contribute to the common good of society. This is their perspective.

Clearly this juridical perspective does not encompass everything that is proper to the virtue of justice. Justice is a *moral* virtue—one of the four cardinal virtues, the fundamental virtues of the just person—and as such it includes the rectitude of the human heart. It is also certain that in order for society to develop fully, it needs men and women to be morally upright. Attaining this goal, though, is the joint task of educators, politicians and moralists: ultimately, the one who can best attain this end is the one with religious experience. On the other hand, only the aspect of justice belongs to the jurist: the realisation of its object, the result that corresponds to the virtue. In other words, his objective is to determine the *external activity* of justice without entering into the interior places of the heart of the one who acts—a matter which he leaves to the moralist. Likewise, *with respect to their fulfillment*, laws are limited to external activity; they thus conform themselves to and show consideration for humans as good citizens with respect to legal justice and in order to be at peace with society. Obtaining everything else is proper to the *other resources* of the human community, especially education and religious experience.

Precisely because society needs men and women to be morally upright, laws must favour education, morality and religion. There are *permissive laws* which are not those that tolerate some social vice in order to avoid a greater evil (or *tolerant laws*) but those which elevate what is immoral to the legal level, accepting them as a social rule. Permissive laws are contrary to the good of society, and they constitute a grave political error. Nevertheless, law as such does not demand integral morality of conduct in order to comply with it but conformity with it in terms of external compliance. Immoderately desiring the goods of others is evil and constitutes an immoral act, but for the law it is sufficient that the citizen not cross over into the field of action by robbing, defrauding or stealing.

## 5.  Relationship between law and legislation

As we have already seen, the jurist can be called *a man/woman of laws [leyes]*. And we have also observed that legislation does not constitute the primary object of the art of the jurist. The art of the jurist consists of discerning what the law *[derecho]* is, what is just. Therefore, if the jurist studies legislation, he does so because it has a strict relationship with the law. In order to know about the law, it is necessary to know about legislation.

The relationship between law and legislation is so intimate that one of the first things noticed is the age-old custom of identifying law with legislation. This is said indiscriminately of penal law and penal legislation, administrative law and administrative legislation, etc. Moreover, it almost always happens that one hears another speaking about law, and it is soon realised that he is speaking about legislation.

At the beginning of this book, we alluded to normativism, that posture which reduces law to legislation; it is clear that, for normativists, identifying law with legislation is the most natural thing in the world. It is not evident, though, that normativists are to be blamed for identifying law with legislation; this manner of speaking was common many centuries earlier, even with the Roman jurists. We had earlier alluded to the fact that this phenomenon is explained by the translation of the language used; we will now elaborate on this explanation.

*Analogy of attribution* holds the blame for identifying law with legislation. This is very easy to understand. There are things that are similar even while being distinct. They are not equal; they are distinct, but *they are related to each other*. For example, it is said of paintings at an exposition that they were an *explosion* of colour, that there was an *explosion* of enthusiasm within the general public that saw them, and that everything ended in disgrace because of the *explosion* of a bomb; I have used the word explosion in three different senses, but they are *related* senses with a common foundation. With respect to colour, enthusiasm and bombs, the explosion is not explosion in the same manner—it is not the same thing; nevertheless, there exists a similarity between the three senses which the term explosion acquires in order to be applied to colour, enthusiasm and a bomb. The relationship of similarity among the three ideas expressed by the word explosion is an *analogy of attribution*.

Let us observe that, of the three similar meanings of the word explosion which we have considered, one expresses what an explosion is in its primary sense; the others are applications which we make to other things due to their likeness with this primary sense. Well then, properly speaking, an explosion is that of a bomb, that is, the crashing of a body or receptacle for the transformation of the substance contained in it into gases. The term employed according to this primary sense is called the *compared* word, and the rest are called *analogous* words.

If one understands these remarks, the following affirmation will be immediately understood: law [*derecho*], in the sense of what is just, is the term compared to, and law [*derecho*] in the sense of legislation is the analogous word. Since it can happen that some readers may not be used to this way of speaking, though, we are going to explain it in other words.

A *right* [*derecho*], just as we said before, is something which is attributed to a subject; we have said that a right is what is just or what belongs to each one. Legislation is something different: it is an obligatory rule of conduct. One may look at it however he wants, but legislation is something distinct from a right. It happens, though, that legislation is a *cause* and *measure* of rights, since there is a double proportion between rights and legislation: that which exists between a cause and an effect (e.g., every person leaves his mark or his style on whatever he does; hence, by looking at writing, graphoanalysts can perceive certain character traits of the person), and that which exists between a measure and what is measured (e.g., between a mould and that which is moulded). We already have the foundation of the analogy: rights are also called legislation by analogy. Now then, the term rights applied to legislation is *analogous* (it does not mean *what is just*, but *the cause and measure of what is just*) and *analogised* (legislation is called a right only by its relationship to what is just). The word "rights" is applied to legislation by analogy of attribution.

## 6. Cause and measure of rights

It is now time, though, to explain the relationship between rights and legislation. With respect to rights, legislation has the two functions to which we just alluded. The first of these is that of being a cause of rights. Although other things can also cause rights—e.g., contracts, human nature—there is no doubt that written or unwritten legislation (the latter is called *custom* or customary law) is a means by which certain things are attributed to determined subjects. Legislation allots things with titles of attribution, which have the character of requirement and indebtedness: they create rights [*derechos*]. So for example, constitutional legislation attributes respective functions to organs of government.

No less important is the function which establishes legislation as a *measure* of rights. Being a measure is equivalent to being a norm or a rule of a legal system; in other words, legislation governs rights and the way to use them: it indicates their limits, prescribes requirements for capacity, establishes systems of guarantee, etc.

The importance which knowledge of legislation has for the jurist is easily understood. Rights are understood by means of legislation, although legislation may not be the only thing that he must take into account. Hence, the jurist can reasonably be called *a man/woman of laws* [*leyes*], and the study of law [*derecho*] is customarily called the *study of laws* [*leyes*]; similarly, some time ago, Law faculties were called faculties of Legislation, and some are so called still in several countries.

At the same time, though, the jurist must be aware that his mission is not to be at the service of legislation—"the law is the law"—but at the service of rights; he is not a functionary of legislation, but a servant of justice in favour of society. Undoubtedly, the jurist has to seek the sense of a piece of legislation, and he has to abide by what legislation prescribes; but he has to interpret it as a function of law, that is, of what is just in the concrete case.

Little more needs to be said of legislation (in an introduction like this) with respect to its *juridical* facet, with respect to its relationship with the law. Nevertheless, it is also important to ponder its *political* facet, while examining the other aspects of legislation which the jurist must understand.

# Chapter VII

# Law in Society

## 1. A rule of good citizenship

It is possible that, in speaking of the "political facet" of laws, one immediately thinks of political parties, elections, and the conduct of politicians for obtaining their objectives. It is good to correct this mistake. The *political* aspect does not refer to these things (at least in a direct and principal way). Politics is the art of governing society, of reaching its ends, of obtaining a peaceful development of the life of peoples and nations—politics understood as something greater than politicking. Law is related to politics in the more noble sense of the word: the art of leading society to the common good.

We said earlier that a law is a norm or obligatory rule of social conduct which marks the portion that belongs to each one in relation to the good of society. It is a rule of *good citizenship* with respect to legal justice. Who is a *good citizen*? A good citizen is one who acts in a manner that assists society in the attainment of its ends, that is, one who contributes to the common good in what pertains to him. We were saying the same thing before in other words: a good citizen is one who complies with the portion which concerns him in relation to the common good of society. And so a rule of good citizenship (with respect to justice) is a law. This situates us before the function of laws, which is nothing other than making persons good citizens.

Nevertheless, we do not think that the law makes good citizens like education does—that is, morally forming them; but it, too, partially fulfills this function. A law is not a moral opinion, nor is a Code a treatise on ethics. The law makes good citizens according to justice *by regulating their social, external conduct*. One becomes a good driver by apprenticeship and practice; on the other hand, the law makes *good drivers* in the sense of marking (by means of commands) what each driver must do in different circumstances. When all drivers comply with the Traffic Code, the result is easy, fluid and correct traffic (relative social order), and hence it refers to *good citizenship* in this aspect.

This undoubtedly means that laws model to society, and consequently to the citizens, a *plan* for society. Laws presuppose in the legislator an idea about society or about the concrete subject matter which is the object of a law. This plan or model of society often flows from society itself by means of the development of social life, which is based on customs. Other times, it concerns a social project which has its origins in minority ideologies. In the latter case, laws can provoke tensions, even grave ones, if they produce the resistance of the social body.

For this reason, the art of making laws, which is part of political prudence, always takes into account the real situation of society, which is part of the *social reality*. It does not attempt rapid or spectacular changes—which do not usually turn out, except in very rare historical circumstances—nor does it happen by large leaps. It relies on the law of gradual progress and gradual change. This is because every law, for compliance, establishes in citizens the corresponding habits—practices and customs. Creating these habits and introducing other new ones does not happen in a day; it takes time and effort. If law governs the life of citizens in a manner very alien to that which had been governing them thus far, the result is violent conflict, which usually ends with the failure of the legislator.

On a small scale, we all have experience of how changes in secure rules of conduct immediately produce a certain disorder, and not until later are new habits formed. For example, if the routes and stops of city buses are changed, it often happens that, even if sufficient warning was given, there are not a few passengers who are disoriented and confused during the initial days of the change; even after a few months one can find people who are thrown off, people who, because of habit, wait in vain for the bus at the old stop or confuse buses. The same happens when traffic directions for cars are modified—

bureaucratic procedures or things of this sort. If this happens on a small scale, it is easy to imagine what follows when changes which affect important aspects of the model of society are introduced. We cannot be surprised that a few years after democracy was restored in Spain, there were many who were lamenting the persistence of non-democratic habits among politicians and citizens. In things of this nature, only a long time gives consistency to mentalities and behaviour.

Compliance with laws comes by creating mentalities and habits in the citizen; it often goes unnoticed that the citizen conforms himself to laws and accommodates himself to them such that the law makes *good citizens* (or bad ones if the law is bad).

## 2.   Interpretation of law and social reality

The social fact just described emphasises how necessary is patience in politicians and prudence in jurists. Since this is not an introduction to political science but the science of law, we will leave the question of patience aside and instead add some words about the prudence of jurists.

Applying laws in accord with social reality forms a part of juridical prudence—of the art of law or jurisprudence. This does not entail scoffing at the law or, at the same time, of introducing disturbances into social life. Law regulates and conforms social reality, and social life must therefore be accommodated to the law; on the other hand, the law could remain unobserved. Popular wisdom, however, would say that "the enemy of what is good is what is better." The jurist must have the acumen of knowing how far he can reach in applying the law, which is the element of accommodating the social reality; thus, in applying the law, the law serves as a factor of order and progress and not of disturbance. When it becomes a disturbance, law ceases to be reasonable, and it becomes a factor that corrupts social order.

This accommodation of law to social reality supposes a progressive accommodation of social reality to laws, such that there may be situations in which the law finds itself further along than social reality. In not a few cases, though, social reality is more evolving and progressive than laws. When this occurs, the *progressive interpretation* of laws emerges; they are applied in accord with the evolution of social reality, allowing for the laws themselves to be at the service of the good of society without severing the relationship of law and reality. This explains how some laws may themselves be able to endure the ages without needing to be changed.

In our time, we are so used to changes that we can scarcely appreciate the value of the *stability* of laws. Nevertheless, and without at all exaggerating—for rigidity does not form part of the prudence of the jurist but rather his imprudence—stable laws are a great benefit, and this is usually an indication of wisdom in legislators and peoples. The reader may wonder which is enviable, though: the political stability of North America, which has had a Constitution for 200 years (keeping in mind that the United States is one of the most evolving societ- ies), or the instability of Spain, which, since 1812, has had eight or ten constitutions—depending upon whether one considers some of the fundamental laws to be constitutional—besides some reforms (there is no absence of those who already wish to introduce some changes into the Constitution of 1978). When one perceives peoples with great stabil- ity in their constitutions, remarks are made about their political wisdom; and the same happens with other laws. Certainly the time comes when laws must be amended, reformed or changed, and this also forms part of the wisdom of a people or legisla- tor; but the instability of laws or their frequent amendment or reform is not good. The adaptation of laws has to be a work principally of progressive interpretation. (Who questions whether the Ameri- can Constitution has undergone an adaptation to the times and the addition of amendments?)

At this point it is very possible that a question may be stirring in the reader's mind. We have spo- ken of an adaptation of social reality to laws and of an adaptation of laws to social reality. Is this not a contradiction? What must be adapted to what? The truth is that there is no contradiction between the two. Social reality is regulated by the law, and in this sense it is social life which adapts itself to law; but on the other hand, this regulation must be done such that social life is developed in accord with its state and conditions. An example can serve to clarify. In order to correct a child's flat feet, it is common to use orthopaedic shoes. The characteristic of these shoes is such that, when one walks, the form of the shoes exerts pressure on the sole of the foot, and they curve the corresponding bone until it obtains its normal form. Law can be compared to these orthopaedic shoes; its function is to regulate, to channel the social reality, and to make it conform to a determined form. As an orthopaedic shoe does for a foot, so law must give form to a regulated society. Now then, it is no less certain that an orthopaedic shoe must be suited to the foot. If the patient wears size 5, size 9 shoes cannot be given to him no matter how orthopaedic they may be; besides, he would look like a clown, and they would injure him more than cure him. So also must the law correspond to the situation proper to the social reality.

## 3.   Law and the common good

We have already seen that the *function* of laws is to make good citizens, and later on we will return to this question. At this time, though, instead of continuing with the theme of good citizenship, it would be better to explain what the *goal* of laws is. To what are laws directed? Why are they preoccupied with making good citizens?

Laws are an instrument of the political art consisting of general and obligatory rules or norms which order social life by regulating behaviour and establishing or organising distinct social structures.

Also, the art of politics is the art of governing society, and governing consists of leading the governed things to their end. The captain rules the ship by leading it to the port from departure to arrival. Consequently, the end of the art of politics is the same as that of society, that which we recognise with the name "common good." This and nothing else is the end of laws; laws are rules which order social life with respect to the common good.

For the present, this has an important consequence: laws do not exist for the particular benefit of politicians or specific social groups composed of citizens. The government which falls into the vice of governing for the private benefit of those who govern or for that of groups of individuals illegitimately exercises its functions; it is a government that is illegitimate with the *illegitimacy of exercise*. Likewise, laws which have this defect are unjust laws. This is a fundamental criterion for evaluating the legitimacy of political regimes and of governments. Legitimacy does not depend only on the political regime adopted—which can vary depending on the historical circumstances through which a country may pass—but also on the exercise of governance in favour of the common good. When a government works in favour of the common good of society and respects the natural rights of persons, its legitimacy of exercise is undoubted, and the question of the *form of government* or of *regime* is situated within the order of political preference and within that of justice.

For their part, laws have to be directed to the common good; they have to establish what is in the general interest of society. This does not mean that laws cannot grant certain benefits to individuals. Not a few laws do this: for example, subsidies for determined companies, credit breaks for farmers, tax exemptions for foundations and non-profit corporations, etc.; but these are benefits that redound to the common good. For instance, if farm prices are subsidised, it must be because it is in the common interest that the agriculture of a country not deteriorate; otherwise, there would be the crime of embezzling public funds. Without being motivated by the common good, the goal of laws would be destroyed since laws directed to satisfy individual interests would be unjust. This is an aspect more of rendering an account in order to avoid deception; at times it seems to us as citizens that the government and laws may be obliged to resolve our personal problems. We might desire a kind of providence-State which cares for our individual happiness, which attends to our desires and personal hopes, and we often complain that it does not do so. Our complaint is not reasonable. We must resolve and attend to our personal problems and individual interests; for we are adults endowed with intelligence and, above all, autonomy and freedom. Seeking the protection and providence of the State for our individual affairs is to renounce our condition as free persons, begging for a collectivism which depersonalises. Like the State and the government, laws exist in order to obtain the general well-being, common happiness or, if one prefers, the necessary and fitting social conditions for citizens to attain their personal development. We allude to *personal development* in order to emphasise that the common good and the general interest are ultimately at the service of the person; laws and society do not neglect the good of the individual and the person. This is certain, but its mission finds its end in those *social conditions that are necessary and fitting*; then, it is the person, the family and smaller communities which must become the protagonists of these. This means that laws and society look toward the good of persons, but they also do not invade the boundaries of others.

One consequence of this goal of laws is that, by being directed toward the common good, laws are concerned with what is general in society, such that they can harm individual interests in some cases. When this happens, it is necessary to know how to distinguish between two different situations. It sometimes happens that there is conflict between the general interest and the individual interest of some citizens; thus, for instance, declaring some plots of land to be green zones or agricultural territory can prejudice the economic interests of the owners since their worth may become quite diminished. There are situations which have no better solution than to sacrifice the individual interest for a general interest; one naturally has to try to avoid this possibility unless there is no alternative.

Nevertheless, there can be another distinct circumstance which is due not to the goal of laws but to the general character found in the language with which they were drafted. The legislator cannot foresee all potential cases to which a law seems to apply; in drafting it, therefore, he takes into account what usually happens and not particular situations. In these particular situations, the law can present aspects whose application leads to resolutions which may turn out to be excessively rigorous or which bring prejudice on that which the law means to defend. What should one do in these cases? It is necessary that one not fall into the argument of the petty lawyer: "the law is the law" or *dura lex sed lex*.[7] The law must be interpreted and applied more in its spirit than according to its letter. This way of interpreting the law is called *equitable*, and the virtue which produces it receives the name of *equity*.

## 4. Rationality of law

The foundation of equity lies in the fact that laws have to be understood as *reasonable* rules. This is a basic characteristic referring to law, its application, and the use of rights: they must be reasonable. Hence, one of the most necessary features of the jurist is that he has *common sense*. It could be said that the art of the jurist is the art of common sense applied to legal questions as well as the art of justice. Hence, it is not surprising that in a university going through difficult times, students of Law may be distinguished for their balanced positions, and they may scarcely be given over to extremist views (in general; there are always

---

7. Translator's note: "The law is tough, but it's the law."

exceptions); they are usually rather reasonable, having sufficient common sense, not yielding themselves to illusory and excessive positions. The art which they have learned teaches them that it is necessary in social life to act according to reason and with moderation, with rationality.

There are two ways to behave oneself in life: with respect to aspects of one's personal life and with respect to aspects of one's political and social life. One posture consists of living as one may wish: I may do the things *which I want and because I want to*. This is a voluntaristic attitude, which gives primacy to what the will desires. It is customarily said of persons who so act that *they do not listen to reason*. In reality we all on occasion act in this manner; we do something not because it is good or evil but because our will is attached to it; and if someone reproves us, it is easy for us to get angry and say that we are doing this "because I feel like it." This voluntaristic attitude not infrequently applies to those who give orders. One obeys them not because it is reasonable to obey what they command but only because they command it. The boss is the boss. And it can happen that the one who commands may adopt this attitude as well: those subject to his command must obey, no matter what he commands, for the simple reason that they are his commands. It is required by the will of the boss. This fatal attitude can be generalised and elevated to the category of a philosophy or theory of human conduct, social power, or laws. And in fact, centuries ago the philosophical theory called *voluntarism* emerged. According to voluntarism, laws express the will of the legislator. Commanding consists of the capacity—granted by the law, won by force, or spontaneously accepted by a group—of imposing one's will; it is an act of the will which contains a desire. In some cases, commanding will be legitimate, and in others it will not; but it always consists of an act of the will.

According to voluntarism, laws express the will of the legislator and are valid as an expression of this will. Does this have consequences for understanding and interpreting laws? It does, and they are very important. In accord with voluntarism, the interpreter of the law must limit himself to capturing the will of the legislator without raising questions about its rationality. He who obeys must comply with what the legislator has wished, regardless of whether it is good or evil. Carrying the idea further still, in reality there are not things that are good or evil in themselves but those which are good inasmuch as they are desired by the one who commands and evil inasmuch as they are rejected by him. It is a known fact that this voluntaristic mentality is that which explains how laws as erroneous as those of the Nazis could be applied by most judges in Hitler's Germany—judges who, aside from this, were personally neither better nor worse than those of other countries. Perhaps the reader does not believe that voluntarism is a theory of our times or thinks it is applicable only to the example which we have proposed. It is a very old theory, and there is even no absence of Medieval authors who applied it to the Ten Commandments; lying, stealing, killing, etc. are not evil in themselves but only because God has prohibited them according to his free will; he could have commanded that we hate our neighbour, that we may rob or murder him, etc. For voluntarism, there are not things that are good or evil in themselves but things that are prescribed or prohibited by he who commands, since the Decalogue is an expression of the free will of God. With these ideas, if one omits God, one necessarily falls into a *juridical positivism*. Every law, inasmuch as it comes from a legislator—even if it is absurd or unjust, to use the words of positivists themselves—is valid and true law. Consequently, humans have no true rights that pre-exist the law, and the whole juridical order has the dictates of law as its sovereign point of reference. If two persons enter a contract, the contract is valid because the law gives it juridical effects; if a custom produces a rule of law, it is because the legislator consents to it. And ultimately the whole art of the jurist is summed up in submitting facts to the assertions of the law.

Voluntarism—and its fruit, positivism—is allied not only with totalitarian forms of government. We have also seen that it can be a personal attitude, and it is a philosophical theory compatible with democratic government as well. In a democracy marked with voluntarism, the legislator is different than that of totalitarian regimes, but the way of understanding laws is not. In democracy, the key aspect is what is called the dogma of *popular sovereignty*. No criterion of good or evil exists beyond the dictates of the majority, the will of the people. Morality and natural law are substituted by *polls*; the criterion which the legislator must follow is what polls demonstrate to be the opinion of the majority.

Just as in the depths of each person it is pleasing to us to do what we want, voluntarism has never failed to have proponents, and in our time it has many of them. There is only one "minor" detail: things are not as we want them to be but as they are. It might be pleasing to all of us that the fire that serves to roast the meat when we have a barbeque with our friends be respectful of our body if we find ourselves enwrapped in its flames. The strength and steel rigidity of a lock on a door seems to be secure to the one who installed it; it hinders undesirable people from entering the closed dwelling, but he curses it if, through an oversight, it keeps him locked inside; and on that occasion he wishes with his whole being that the steel were as soft as butter. Our will is *capricious* (*blind*, the philosophers say) and things are not; they have laws that govern them. Things are as they are. Hence, humans must act *according to things*, in accord with the laws—with the order—which govern them. When humans do this, they can have dominion over their environment, and things serve them. If they respect the laws of the universe, humans can fly and even reach the moon; if they do not respect them, they provoke harmful consequences; they will get hurt or even killed. Acting in conformity with the order that governs things is to act *rationally*—that is, according to reason, which is what understands this order and dictates to each one what he or she must do in accord with it.

And so, humans *are as they are*—not only on the physical and biological plane but also on the moral plane. In the moral realm, human beings are neither capricious nor purely free. Humans are persons, and by being persons they carry dignity; they have a specific manner of being which necessitates (as we saw earlier) that there are things in their activity that are good or evil in themselves, independently of what is pleasing or displeasing to them, of what they may or may not want. And here—even more force-fully than with physical things—our will is capri-cious: we think it is very wrong for others to deceive us, but we would like it if our lies were not morally evil; abortionists can loudly demand abortion, but they call out with no less force if someone kills one of their own or simply mistreats someone. The fol-lowing popular saying is appropriate vis-à-vis this attitude: "Either we respect everyone, or we start a fight."[8] These demands—which, in themselves and with respect to others, flow from the personal nature of humans—are what constitute the moral order and the *natural* juridical order which is expressed in *nat-ural law*. The person is a being who by his or her nature is fulfilled by knowledge and love; hence, the

---

8. Translator's note: *O jugamos todos o rompemos la baraja*—literally, "Either we play all [the cards] or we destroy the deck."

truth and the good constitute his or her *objective* rule and goal. Based *objectively* on these—what is one's own, independently of what may or may not be desired—people act like people; if one acts contrary to these, one debases oneself. In the same way, based on these, human society attains its purposes or otherwise becomes decadent and inhuman. This moral and natural juridical order is known by reason and is expressed in the form of pronouncements and judgements which contain commands ("it is necessary to do this"), permissions ("it may be done in this way"), or prohibitions ("this must not be done"). By following this moral and juridical order, man acts *reasonably*.

The laws of society (those which we have called *laws* without further specification) must also be rational. Moreover, they exist and are justified as the rational dictates of the legislator. By their nature, they are *dictates of reason* which establish a social order determined among various possibilities in conformity with things as they are. This has an important consequence: just as humans are persons whose being demands that they act in certain specific ways and that they be treated not according to caprice but in accord with their natural rights (of which we have already spoken), laws are either rational or they become an illegitimate influence in the social order. We as persons are not to be commanded or treated as the legislator may wish but as persons; otherwise, "start a fight"; let the legislator follow his "laws." We are persons before we are citizens.

Without being preoccupied about extremes by having to start a fight, the jurist must always interpret the law *reasonably*, according to what is rational and what ends up being reasonable in each moment, precisely because this is demanded by the internal rational character of laws. Hence, the interpreter of the law does not look only at the law; he also fixes his gaze on the social reality and the circumstances of the concrete case, and he *reasonably* applies the law to the case. Hence, when the law produces harmful effects in a concrete case, he has recourse to equity. Jurists are reasonable people, and they always suppose that the legislator is, too. (And if he is not, they try to make him reasonable, because the good of persons and society always comes before the caprice of the legislator.)

Oh, I have been forgetting myself! Just as the attitude of giving primacy to the will is called *voluntarism* when it is raise to the level of a theory, so the attitude of behaving oneself rationally is called *intellectualism* if one makes it a theory.

## 5.   Competent authority

We have seen that if laws are not directed toward the common good and are not rational, we as citizens are permitted "to start a fight," not to enter into the game. Said otherwise, laws are *able to be obeyed* when their content is *legitimate*. The legitimacy of laws, though, is not exhausted by their content; in order to oblige citizens, it is necessary that they proceed from a competent authority. Everybody cannot issue laws, as we know. We would all like to impose the laws that we like upon society, but we also know that this would be a vain pretension. If a certain citizen were to dedicate himself to promulgating laws, at first people would be curious about who this strange person was, and the person might even be interviewed on TV; but in the end, either he would be confined to an insane asylum or he would continue to be perceived as a person greatly disturbed in the head. It would occur to no one to take such "laws" seriously. Making laws is not the responsibility of *individuals*. Even if they are very learned and very capable of making excellent laws, the most that individuals can do is to make *drafts* of law. Throughout history there have been great thinkers who have presented a system of laws which they believed to be exemplary for society. Plato and Cicero have produced such works that are rightfully renowned; and others have done so as well. This is what they are, though: books of philosophy or political thought, not laws. If the government decides to construct some public roads, make some bridges, or install some railroads, it usually makes an agreement with a company by which it accomplishes these activities. On the other hand, it cannot entrust to a company the issuing and promulgating of laws; such a commission would lack force. With some frequency, the one who is charged with legislating entrusts the *drafting* of law to pre-eminent jurists; this has been done with such great legislative texts as the Digest and *Pandectæ* of Justinian, the Decretals of Gregory IX, or the Code of Napoleon. Jurists, however, had and have the material task of compiling or composing the texts. The weight of the law in force, though, emanates from the legislator who promulgates the laws. This is why they are known by the name of legislator—he is their author—and not by the name of the jurist or jurists who materially composed them. The Decretals were compiled by Saint Raymond of Peñafort, but as a legislative text its author was Pope Gregory IX, and it was and is known by his name, even if he did no more than write his signature on the bull of promulgation.

Laws are rules of the conduct of citizens and of the organisation of society, whose purpose is the common good. They are what indicate the portion of each one in relation to social ends; therefore, issuing laws does not pertain to individuals but to the one who has the function of ordering society toward the common good, to the one who has the governance of society. Each country possesses its own legislative organs: Parliament, the King or President, etc. In Spain, Parliament passes laws and the King gives them his royal sanction; the King with the President of the Government signs decree-laws; in addition to the royal signature, decrees bear the signature of the corresponding Minister; each Minister makes ministerial orders, etc. Now is not the time to enter into these details, though, but only to emphasise the point from a general perspective.

Issuing laws belongs to the one who has the duty of directing social life. And since this direction consists of ordering it toward the common good, it belongs to society itself—by itself or by means of its governmental organs. Sometimes the whole society issues laws, and it does this in two ways. One of these is by means of formalised acts such as legislative acts: the referendum and the plebiscite. Other times, laws arise from society by *custom*; with the established requirements being fulfilled, when a practice or custom of acting in a certain manner is created, this custom becomes law [*ley*]. The human community's capacity to produce laws does not arise from a previous law given by one who has power in society, as certain modern authors maintain. Rather, it is an *innate* capacity which belongs to the community as the primary subject of the power of self-governance. Distinct from this is the fact that the faculty to issue laws which is proper to the community is regulated, and some specific requirements for its exercise are imposed (as also happens with acts of governmental organs).

This form of producing laws is not the most common. Each community has its specific governmental organs, among whose faculties the issuing of laws or norms of different degrees is prominent. In such cases, laws emanate from the one who governs society. We could say that the most important function of the one governing is that of giving society good laws, since these are what mark the standards for society, what lead citizens toward the social goal, and what exemplify and typify social life. Laws give backbone and structure to society, such that it can well be said that society will be as its laws are.

## 6.   The legislative process

Laws are instituted—that is, they begin to be laws or obligatory rules—when they are *promulgated*; hence the fundamental act in the process of the production of a law is its *promulgation*. The law, we would say, proceeds from reason. When our reason acts in the practical order (*practical reason*), it is capable of discovering and inventing possible rules of human activity and social organisation. Laws are first a project, and they pass through a process of elaboration, consisting of discovering a possible norm, discussing it, improving it, etc. Because of the means of communication, we are all aware of this process. The cabinets of study in public organs or political parties, commissions named for this purpose or other institutions or groups of this sort compose the first draft. This draft in due time is studied by Parliament in corresponding Commissions, and it finally passes to the Plenary Body of Congress and the Senate. During this whole process, the law is *a draft* (a rough draft, a pre-draft, a first draft, a second draft, etc.). Finally, the law is approved. Up to this point there has been in operation the *rational process* of considering and fixing attention upon the text of the law and the *decision* about whether it may become a law. However, it is still not a law. It will begin to be a law when the one who has this function carries out the act of *communicating* it to society, that act or procedure by which the law comes to be *imposed* upon society as a law. This act is called *promulgation*, and it is accomplished by means determined beforehand, such that there may be no doubt about the existence and content of the law. In Spain, the laws of State organs are promulgated by means of their insertion into the official newspapers called *The Madrid Gazette* and the *Official Bulletin of the State*.[9]

Once the law is promulgated, an interval of time is usually left open so that interested parties may be informed and take the appropriate measures. During this time, the law—which is already law—has suspended its obligatory force; it does not exercise its function, so to speak, just as we describe vacations: this period is called a *vacatio legis*, or a suspensive period of the law. When the period is ended, the law *enters into force*; it begins its *effectiveness*, that is, it obliges with all its effects. The suspensive period of laws in our country is commonly 20 days, but it can be less (or more). And given the haste with which they are sometimes introduced by our politicians, it is not rare of late that laws are suspended no longer than a day; citizens may be left without that deserved rest, having only one day available for reading and becoming informed about it.

9. Translator's note: The publications to which the author refers are the *Gaceta de Madrid* and the *Boletín Oficial del Estado* (B.O.E.). In each country there are publications with this aim: in Canada the federal Government makes the promulgations in the *Canada Gazette*; each province also has its own *Gazette*. Universal canonical legislation is promulgated in the *Acta Apostolicæ Sedis* (c. 8, §1).

# Chapter VIII

# Laws and the Human Person

## 1. Premises

Now that we have considered laws in general and laws within society, it is fitting that we say something about the influence of laws over the human person. In other words, we have to speak about the relationship between laws and morality. With this we are not departing from the object of this book; on the contrary, we are entering into a subject which has special importance for the man/woman of laws to the extent that laws will tend to engage his or her attention more frequently than it may at first seem. The jurist is not to be one who goes his own way, wishing to be only an expert in legal mechanisms and not a jurist. By trade, the jurist is a humanist; he possesses a knowledge whose object is humans within society, and he therefore possesses an art which is ultimately ordered toward the human person. We hereby resume the questions of good citizenship and the function of laws.

Earlier we were saying that laws make good citizens by conforming them in their good external behaviour. We were also saying that the jurist is not a moralist, since by trade he is interested in the *work* of justice, without entering into the intentions which realise this work. All of this is true, but it is of primordial importance that there be no confusion on this point. It was observed before that, since our concern is to know the *political* facet of laws, our intent has been to address this aspect, not limiting ourselves therefore strictly to what laws contain with respect to *rights*, that is, the cause and measure of rights (what is just). Now then, the relationship of laws, in their political aspect, with morality is not the same as the relationship between politics and morality, which was discussed earlier; politics and ethics are not related in the same way as the science of law and the science of morality. Moreover, authors of the philosophy of law frequently fail to distinguish what is juridical and what is political in laws; rather, with the terms *law* and *juridical* they mix both of these aspects of legislation. Let us try to understand the reason for this and, if possible, to see a clear distinction.

One who has the occasion to read manuals of the history of juridical and political thought (there are excellent ones) is left with the idea that, before the 18th century, morality and law were confused; and there was an author of the Enlightenment—with precedents in Hobbes and some others—called Christian Thomasius who separated law and morality.

When reading him, though, it is necessary to be aware of two things: the first is that, before the 18th century, morality and law were not understood as Thomasius defined them; the problem was presented in a different way. Still, jurists were never confused with moralists, except in one period of the High Middle Ages dominated by the theory of *political Augustinianism* in which almost everything was confused (the Church and the State, laws and morality, guilds and confraternities, etc.). In the second place, it must be observed that, when Thomasius and his followers separated what they understood to be morality and law (which was not the earlier understanding of these), they confused law with legislation, and what is juridical about legislation with what is political about legislation. At the beginning, then, being left as an entangled skein, the question of the relationship between morality and law was transformed into an intricate labyrinth.

It is not now the time to attempt to resolve such a difficult problem; but if the reader is inspired to accompany me along the path which follows, I will try to help him not remain caught in the entangled threads of the skein and pass through the labyrinth as gracefully as possible. Let us begin the trip.

## 2. The nature of things and the nature of the sciences

The first precaution that must be taken (an elementary one) is to recall that the sciences and the arts *do not obtain* their objects. They do not intend to grasp them or realise them in their whole potentiality, because they know that this is not possible. They are limited to pondering their objects or to realising them in *one aspect* or from *one perspective*, leaving the rest to other areas of knowledge. For realists, they are modest. For instance, acetylsalicylic acid is of interest to a physician inasmuch as it relieves a headache; but it does not belong to the condition of a physician to know its molecular structure or the manufacturing processes or the problems of marketing this substance; for these, there are physicists, chemists, and entrepreneurs. The physician is not a chemist, even though both study the same substance; one understands how to make acetylsalicylic acid and the other knows when it is necessary to prescribe it as medication. This fact leads us to avoid confusing the thing that is the object of knowledge with the perspective from which it is studied, and to avoid believing that one science tells us everything about a thing, since it only speaks to us of one *aspect*.

Since the same thing can be studied by different sciences, it is not necessary to confuse *the nature of things* with the *nature of the sciences*. Human behaviour, for example, can be studied by the philosophical sciences, like moral philosophy, and by the experimental sciences, like empirical sociology. Hence, the *moral life*—a reality of a moral nature—can be the object of various sciences. Not every science which studies the moral life has to be part of moral philosophy—a clear example of this being empirical sociology, which we just mentioned. With this we arrive at the first conclusion: the question of whether the jurist is a moralist—whether the science of law is part of moral philosophy or moral theology—does not accomplish the same thing as asking whether *law* is or is not a *moral reality*.

The second precaution consists of not confusing law with legislation. It is one thing to investigate whether law is of a moral nature, and it is another to elucidate whether legislation pertains to the moral order.

## 3. Moral reality

Having made these preliminary observations, the first question to explain is whether law and legislation are of a *moral nature*; we are in the realm, not of the sciences but of realities.

What do we call the moral order or the order of moral realities? There are those who understand that the moral order is the order of human conduct in relation to God or, from another point of view, the order of the relationship of the person with him or herself. This definition, though, is prone to *confuse the reality with the perspective of moral philosophy and moral theology*. It is the error into which Thomasius very frequently fell. In effect, the relationship of human persons to God or to themselves—aspects that are true and so fundamental to moral reality—constitute the ultimate and proximate perspectives of these sciences, but they do not exhaust the whole moral reality. It has been observed that these perspectives concern *the goal* of acts, that is, they refer to the relationship between human behaviour and its ends. Well then, reality is more than its ends; it is clear therefore that such perspectives do not exhaust the whole reality of morality. When a moralist says that *morality* consists of the relationship of human acts with their ends and therefore with the laws that govern them, the word "morality" is taken as a *formality* (therefore, in the strict sense) and not as a bare reality; that is, he speaks of reality seen ultimately from his scientific perspective (this is to what we refer when speaking of formality). This is one of the knots of the skein which must be unwound.

In the order of reality, there exists a plane of the being of persons which is what belongs to their condition as persons, that which manifests in a man or a woman the fact that he or she is endowed with reason, a will, and consequently freedom. The nature of this plane is distinct from those spheres of his or her being governed by physical and biological laws. On the plane of personality, humans act according to their own motives: their acts proceed from their self-determination, from their free decision. This concerns a sector of human reality which has a particular character. In Greece, this particular order of human conduct received the name *ethos*, whence comes the word "ethics"; and in Rome, it was called "what is proper to custom," or *mos* (*mores*, in the plural), and from this the word "moral" is derived.

This plane of human reality is what belongs to men and women as persons—that by which they act and are realised as such. If we account for the fact that the person is fulfilled by knowing and loving, it is easily concluded that, in this order, persons act by reason (intellectual knowledge) and by will (love). *The plane of moral reality or ethics is the plane of the human being's action as a person.* On this plane, the person acts freely, and his/her potentialities are suited for acting well by means of certain particular habits which are called *virtues*, some of which pertain to the *intellect* and others to the *will*.

Now, this moral reality is the object (among others) of three practical sciences which observe the acts of humans as persons according to three distinct perspectives: the science of law (jurist), the moral science (moralist), and the science of politics (politician). For non-moral human realities there are other sciences: medicine, biology, etc.

Is law part of *moral reality*? Without a doubt it is. We have said that the just thing is something that is due; obligation presupposes freedom, and therefore what is just is given by a free decision of the will. Likewise, crime and injustice presuppose freedom (a demented person is not guilty, nor is he unjust). The *giving* to each his own (what is just) is the fruit of a *virtue* of the will: justice. And knowing how to discern what is just as well as when and how it must be given is another virtue: prudence (prudence about rights, or jurisprudence). With respect to rights, humans act as persons; moreover, a right or a just thing presupposes the order of free action. Who can doubt that rights pertain to *moral reality*? In the same way, *political* action (humans' life within society) pertains to the order of *personal* action, of free actions. *Political reality* is a dimension of the *moral reality* of persons. Laws are norms of this free action; their mandatory character especially presupposes freedom, since action that is not free is not commanded; *it is produced* or *induced*. Laws by definition pertain to human moral reality.

Like any other reality of this world, human moral reality is not simple but a composite; it contains *composition* in *unity*. It contains composition, because each act of a moral nature affects the different *relationships* of persons; within moral reality, three types of relationships can be concretely distinguished: of the human being with God, with himself, and with others. For human acts indicate a relationship with the law of God, with the demands of the realisation of one's personal being personal being, and with others. Regarding the third, there are two more distinct forms of relationship: that of justice in itself (a juridical relationship, or one of rights) and as a member of the human community (politics).

And so this composition entails a unity, since it is each act—as a *single* entity—that affects one or all of the relationships mentioned. There are distinct sciences for each composition. In terms of unity, there are aspects which are common to these sciences; for instance, the theme of responsibility and its degrees is unified in its central nucleus.

## 4. Sciences of moral reality

Supposing the unity of moral reality, the existence of distinct relationships brings particular principles and rules of acting to each one of these relationships, and these aid the distinction of areas of practical knowledge *with respect to these relationships*. There thus emerges the formal (principal) element of the distinction of the three areas of practical knowledge regarding moral reality: the science of the jurist (the science or art of law), the science of the politician (the science or art of politics), and the science of the moralist (the science or art of morality proper). On the other hand, just as not all moral or personal acts (human acts) affect all relationships, there is a secondary distinguishing factor or material element: the moralist studies *all* acts, the jurist studies those which refer to relationships of justice, and the politician studies those which are directed toward the common good of society. In what follows, let us define (in very brief strokes) each one of these sciences.

The *moral* science—or the science of the moralist—is so called *par excellence*, not because it studies the moral reality in all its aspects, but because it belongs to the analysis of human conduct in its most fundamental human aspect: according to the demands which flow from the condition of the person. This is usually expressed by saying that it studies the human being's conduct *in relation to himself and God*. A genuine study of morality can be realised with the light of reason alone, and this is called moral philosophy; or it can be studied by taking the data of divine revelation into account, and here it receives the name of moral theology. Although *what is specific* to morality is its relationship with human conduct with respect to the person himself and God, it is for morality to determine common principles and rules of human acts as they are seen in their most fundamental moral aspect. So for example, analysing the elements of human acts, degrees of responsibility, etc. is proper to morality, which for this reason receives this name *par excellence*. Morality, we say, does not study human conduct in all its relationships but only to the extent indicated above; in this sense, it does not study moral reality in all its dimensions. However, since all human conduct stands in relation with the person himself and with God, morality has as its material object every human act; that is, *from this perspective*, it embraces the whole moral subject matter, as well as law and political activity.

The juridical science has a more limited material object; it only encompasses acts of the virtue of justice; and so it is confined to determining the *works* proper to justice. It does not even study the virtue of justice in its entirety, though; it is limited, as we were saying, to the *external* work of justice. Its perspective is understanding a right as something that is due, and its goal consists of each one having what is his own. Its object does not consist of the claim that the human being is fulfilled as a person by being just—this belongs to morality—; it consists of the concern that each person's rights are respected; it is a *social* science, or a science of some determined and specific social relationships. Because of this perspective, the science of law is not one part of morality, and the jurist is not a moralist. Both of them, the jurist and the moralist, study justice, but their perspectives are distinct: it is the concern of the moralist that loans are not usurious, so that humans may conduct themselves as persons and not commit sin (an offense against God by breaking His law); the concern of the jurist regarding loans is the same, but for another reason: in order that the rights of each one may be respected, that each may receive what belongs to him, thus making a just social order.

The political science, for its part, studies human conduct from the perspective of the *common good* of society—not, as is proper to morality, from the point of view of the total good of the person (which ultimately is God), but from the perspective of *social order* or the ordering of society to a common good. Politics is circumscribed by the good functioning of society, by the general and specific conditions which are suitable for the development and progress of the human community. In this sense, it is a science that is distinct from morality; it is not one part of moral philosophy. One clear relationship exists between ethics, morality and politics, though—a relationship which we are going to study briefly in the context of laws.

As we have seen, the *political reality* is an aspect of the human *moral reality*; man/woman develops his/her social progress as a person, making use of

knowledge and will. Hence, the social relationship
is not a mere co-existence of individualities, nor can
politics be understood only as a technique for limiting the spheres of freedom and the contribution of
material goods. Although being a *good citizen* does
not entirely coincide with being a *morally good person*—e.g., one can be a great benefactor to society for
reasons of personal vanity, which has little moral
value from the point of view of morality—it tends to
involve the exercise of virtues, at least to a certain
degree. (The benefactor in the example will exercise
freedom, although he may simultaneously be vain.)
Since the social life is a moral reality, *good* citizenship
necessarily has to be the fruit of virtues, even if it
may only reach a certain degree. The reason is simple and clear: in the moral sphere (that of freedom),
good activity is achieved by habits of specifically
*personal* human potencies, which are called virtues:
prudence with respect to practical reason, and justice, fortitude and temperance on the part of the will.
The person has no other way to act in the moral
sphere. Hence, although good citizenship does not
encompass all that is necessary for *good human-ness*,
it is based (at least partially) on the exercise of the
virtues. And so, even though laws contain technical
and organisational aspects, they, too, are ultimately
directed to the citizen's exercise of some specific virtues. Before we proposed the example of the Traffic
Code; without a doubt, the norms of this code have
many technical aspects, but they are ultimately
directed toward making the citizen prudent and
just—that is, so that he may act in a manner that

does not place his own person or others in danger; at times it contributes to each one's ability to employ his right to travel freely. Laws govern the citizen's moral conduct (that is, what is proper to the person as a free and responsible being), even if they are reduced to what has a direct and immediate relationship with the common good without overstepping these limits.

This has a series of consequences which we are going to summarise in order not to inappropriately prolong this small work. They are the following:

*a)* Since laws govern moral conduct—though only by ordering it toward the common good—they are rules of morality, and consequently *they oblige in conscience*. In what sense do they oblige in conscience? They oblige in conscience inasmuch as they are legitimately established rules or measures of acts pertaining to some virtue. Every virtue obliges in conscience, including legal justice; therefore, inasmuch as laws regulate the exercise of a virtue and impose obligations of legal justice, they are obligatory in conscience.

*b)* The art of politics is ultimately directed toward making good citizens, which is inseparable from the virtues. Consequently, laws have to be directed toward promoting and facilitating moral virtues, which implies that laws have to be founded on the *objective moral order*.

*c)* All of human morality does not belong to politics (nor therefore to laws) but only what flows from the *common social good*. Hence, it follows that laws cannot demand more than good citizenship, nor can they penetrate into the sanctuary of the conscience. Hence, with respect to laws, a citizen has *freedom of conscience* just as he has freedom of thought and religious liberty.

*d)* We said above that laws must be accommodated to social reality without attempting to attain the ideal goals all at once. At the same time, we were also saying that laws cannot be limited to shaping in writing what happens in reality (these would not be laws, but sociological constants). By this we mean that laws must tend toward *improving* and *developing* good citizenship; this entails leading citizens toward the exercise of the corresponding virtues; but at the same time, they must begin from the moral state of society. Laws, therefore, cannot demand virtues with all their force, and they can even tolerate some behaviour that is not good.

In this regard one must know how to clearly distinguish tolerant laws from what are called *permissive laws*. A tolerant law begins with the existence of an evil which it is not possible to eradicate without provoking a greater evil; and it is restricted to regulating a situation that is contrary to the common good by trying to limit it as much as the moral state and circumstances of society allow. The tolerance of laws has a clear limitation: laws cannot tolerate any behaviour which directly attacks basic social institutions or the most fundamental rights of persons: the right to life and physical or moral integrity (homicide, abortion, injuries, etc.), freedom (kidnapping), marriage, social authority, etc.

On the other hand, a *permissive law* presupposes the denial of the existence of objective rules of morality, and it consequently *legalises*, that is, issues a statute of social normality for immoral conduct, provided that sufficiently numerous sectors of society request it. This supposes an inversion of the function of law, which thus becomes a vehicle for evil citizenship and immorality. Such laws not only do not oblige in conscience, but acting according to what they permit is contrary to what is moral.

## 5.   Law and moral behaviour

Laws create habits and customs when one acts in conformity with them. For this reason, they are not restricted to making good citizens from the point of view of external conduct; they also influence the morality of persons by contributing to the development of their virtues. Since the majority of virtues are not innate but acquired by the repetition of acts, laws compel one to act according to a virtue and thereby result in the acquisition of the corresponding virtues by the one who obeys them. A driver who complies with the Traffic Code succeeds in possessing the habit of driving prudently; we all have experience that, in virtue of complying with laws, we end up doing by custom—by virtue—many things which are commanded without remembering the law. Here then is one important aspect of the relationship between morality and laws. Laws are not indifferent with respect to the moral formation and moral behaviour of human beings; on the contrary, they greatly influence each other by contributing in a notable manner toward moralising customs (or favouring immorality in the case of permissive, immoral or unjust laws).

Separating *legality* from *morality* as if they were two separate worlds devoid of a mutual relationship supposes a falsified conception of laws, the conception which Thomasius introduced into politics (into legislation)—into law, he claims; and these laws thrive inasmuch as they work toward that utopia of a morally *neutral* State. By their very nature, laws are not and cannot be neutral with respect to morality. When there is the intent to construct a neutral or amoral State and a system of laws that is equally neutral or amoral, in reality an immoral State or immoral laws are introduced, since amorality is a particular form of immorality. It is unnecessary to repeat what is already clear: politics and laws affect the human order of freedom, and in this order human beings are inclined to act virtuously or viciously; there is no alternative. Trying to create politics and laws which do not touch virtues or vices is to fall into the most pure unrealism.

# Chapter IX

# Natural Law and Positive Law

## 1. Introduction

In treatises on the philosophy of legislation—which, beginning with Hegel, are called treatises on the philosophy of law, but the reader already knows that this is based on confusion—one observes a constant and anecdotal coincidence from Aristotle to our time. When they arrive at the point to which we have arrived in this introduction—asking whether there are only laws given by humans or if there is a natural law, connected to the former and at their base—they usually allude to the tragedy of Sophocles called *Antigone* (which is the name of the protagonist). I do not know if this is caused by a gypsy curse or a lack of imagination by philosophers of law. The fact is, neither does it occur to me to begin this section in another way than by relying on the example of *Antigone*, despite the 20 centuries that separate us from Aristotle. And just as it is not due to a belief in gypsy curses nor to being publicly accused of lack of imagination (at any rate, let the reader conclude as he wishes), we are going to say that the great trage- dian Sophocles was successful in leaving imperish- able testimony in his *Antigone* of the fact that natural law exists. However, before paying the inevitable tribute to Sophocles also by referring the words of *Antigone* to the tyrannical Kreon, it seems fitting to explain where this subject comes from.

In the preceding sections, we have spoken about laws (*political* laws, that is, legislation which governs the conduct of citizens in relation to the common good, which legislation can be called jurid- ical insofar as it is the cause and rule or measure of law); and it can occasionally be deduced from the context that legislation has only human society for its author—in itself or by means of competent gov- ernmental organs. The immediately previous sec- tion perhaps supposes that a natural moral law exists—we were speaking of objective moral obliga- tions, of a natural law which regulates the morality of acts, etc.—but it could appear that we just said something which must suppose that there exists a natural law that is *political* (which orders society) or juridical (a rule of law). Such an impression would not be precise. The reality is that we have already addressed this question less systematically; it is cer- tain (it was inevitable) in the preceding pages.

Referring at different moments to natural law, voluntarism, and intellectualism, we were presum- ing that human nature *demands* some specific con- duct, because the human person, in virtue of his dignity and the ends which are proper to him, can neither act entirely as he may wish nor can he be treated according to the free impulsivity of others. We were saying that, in moral reality, there are things which in themselves are right and things which in themselves are evil. Just as politics and the art of law have as their object certain relationships which pertain to the moral order—they are aspects of *moral reality*—the principles which we were just recalling are equally valid for morality, politics and law. We already indicated that moral reality is only one; moral philosophy, the juridical science, and political learning each study different aspects of it. If the reality is one, natural law is consequently one, even if we can distinguish *aspects* in it: as a stream or path of personal realisation, it is a moral law; as the rule or measure of rights, it is a juridical law; and to the extent that it orders society toward the common good, it is the law of the *polis*, or political law.

As we have seen, to the extent that natural rights [*derechos naturales*] exist, juridical law naturally has three facets. In the first place, natural rights obviously have not only a natural title but also a natural measure, as we already indicated. This natural measure or rule of rights is natural law [*ley natural*], since the rule of rights is law [*ley*]. Secondly, the existence of natural rights produces rules of action related to them, even natural ones: "do not kill," "do not steal," "heal the sick," and other more complicated ones. Finally, the nature of social relationships and social institutions entails some rules of commutative, distributive and

legal justice (as the case may be) which are natural—
e.g., food must be distributed such that it reaches
everyone. This complex of rules of law constitutes
the juridical aspect of natural law, or natural juridical
law [*ley*].

There is also a natural political law, or, if it pre-
ferred, natural law also has a political application.
The human community, the society which is shaped
within States and the international community,
relies on a natural principle. By nature, humans are
not only *sociable* (capable of society), but they are
*social* with others. Although there are many possible
*forms* of society, they are all developments of the natural core of society in virtue of which human beings
are by nature united with others by bonds of solidarity and community. We hereby return to a discovery
of the principle to which we referred earlier: every
cultural fact is necessarily a development of a natural datum. Political society would not exist if it did
not depend on a natural core of political association.
Hence, the theory of *social agreement*, according to
which human beings are asocial by nature and
society is the fruit of an agreement among them, has
no sufficient basis; it is impossible. Nothing cultural
is possible for humans—by consent or by agreement
in this case—if a natural basis does not exist. Therefore, if human beings were asocial by nature, society
would not exist since they cannot change their
nature. Since political society is founded on a natural political society, a political natural law necessarily exists: that which indicates the conduct which is

in conformity with this natural reality and the conduct that is contrary to it. Examples of the former are the following: obedience to legitimate authority, the obligation to cooperate for the progress and development of society, the obligation to seek peace and co-existence, respect of the culture of peoples, etc.

Natural moral law, natural juridical law and natural political law are not fashioned as three distinct laws, but they are aspects of one and the same law. Hence, we will now explain the nature and some characteristics of natural law in general, leaving aside for now a more elaborate explanation of the specific details of each one of the aspects mentioned.

## 2.   Truth and opinion

Earlier, in elementary school, we were already hearing talk of natural law, and we doubtless understood it with sufficient depth at the high school and college levels; it was at least sufficient enough that, when we re-discovered it in our study of law or philosophy, we did not have to put forth such excessive efforts to study it; we could dedicate the extra time that we would have needed for understanding it to other subjects, or we could simply spend this time with friends. However, since not everything can be taught in elementary school and at the high school and college levels, and since sociology is now fashionable, it turns out that natural law is usually substituted by *surveys*, since each student declares either what he thinks or how he sees things. Therefore, two objectives are achieved: students arrive at college and university knowing less and less (their professors say this, it is written in newspapers, and the highest educational authorities of the most diverse countries recognise this), and they are accustomed to speak without prior study of that which they are speaking about; logically, they show themselves to be experts in the art of saying nothing. For it turns out that things are not as we think them to be (without studying them) or how we see them (without looking at them) but as they are; and therefore, if we do not acquaint ourselves with what things really are before forming an opinion about them, our opinions amount to a fair of absurdities.

The fact is that, with so many surveys, so much personal opinion, and such a subjective point of view, natural law is usually notably absent from basic general education, even at the college level. And so we are not left with a better remedy than to explain something about it (with brevity, as ever).

Using a phrase that has become common, an illustrious Spanish notary once said that if everyone were in agreement about law, law would be very boring. Indeed, if the degree of boredom with a science is measured by the degree of agreement, there would be no doubt that the juridical science would be very entertaining. This should not be confusing to the reader; it was already noted at the beginning of the book that jurists are not easily found to agree with each other. In the law there are many *disputable* things. And if we pass then to politics, the entertainment increases. It is sufficient to ponder the *alphabet soup* that forms the political spectrum within our purview. Moreover, if we add that not a few divergences are concealed behind each letter, it turns out that politicians must be the least bored group of people in the world. There is undoubtedly an infinity of disputable matters in politics.

It is also true, though, that in morality, in law, and in politics there are things which *are not disputable*; they are as they are. In such cases, an opinion lacks weight unless it serves to oppose the ignorance or wisdom of people. The expressions "I think," "in my personal opinion," and "my point of view" only indicate here the audacity of people to speak about what they do not know or to resolve problems incorrectly, considering something disputable or relative when it is not. For instance, racial discrimination is not a matter of *points of view*. If it were a disputable question that were subject to points of view, the position in favour of racial discrimination would be an opinion just as respectable as any other. As we were saying earlier, if there were only relative values (points of view), nothing would be truly evil or unjust. In politics and in law, as in morality, there are things which do not pertain to *opinion* but to the *truth*, since they are *objective* realities. This complex of objective realities is summarised in *human nature* and in *natural law*.

As we have said, moral reality consists of the sphere of the free activity of persons. And so, freedom finds its primary principle of development and its primary rule of activity in the very being of persons, of which freedom is a characteristic. Freedom *does not make* humans, it is not given to their being; on the contrary, it exists and is developed *by and in the person's being*. In other words, the person's being *is free*; it contains freedom, and it would be false to say that freedom makes the person's being. Man and woman have a free nature, and freedom is therefore based on their nature, untouchable by freedom, because it is a supposition of nature (there would be no freedom without nature). Properly speaking, this nature is a *rule of freedom*, which is the same as saying that freedom finds its meaning and its expression in its development *according to nature*; for it thus fulfills human beings and perfects them. In other words, human nature is normative for human beings' free activity. Therefore, by learning about the person's nature, human reason grasps what is normative for it, and it issues *imperative judgements*: this must be done; that must not be done. The collection of these judgements or imperative rules of human reason— which commands, prohibits, or permits certain behaviour according to its conformity or non-conformity with human beings' nature (their being and their natural ends)—receives the name of *natural law*.

## 3.   Content of natural law

With respect to moral reality, human activity represents the dynamism of the person's being toward its natural ends. Hence, as we just saw, that activity which is in conformity with the ends of the person is in accord with natural law. We know these ends because they are found in our being in the form of *natural inclinations*. We can come to know natural law, then, by perceiving these inclinations. Let us concisely consider what they are, without listing them in any order of importance:

*a*) The inclination toward the preservation of one's being, also called the instinct of preservation. In this regard, we deduce that the life and the physical and moral integrity of man and woman are his and her natural rights, just as health is a natural right. Likewise, that which is opposed to these is contrary to natural law: homicide, injuries, suicide, etc.

*b*) The inclination toward marriage, ordered to the procreation and education of children. From this are deduced the fundamental precepts which govern the institutions of marriage and the family, the rights related to these, the right use of the procreative faculty, etc.

*c*) The inclination toward relationship with God, or religiosity, which gives place to the right of religious liberty, to the moral obligation to seek the truth about God and the worship which is His due, etc.

*d*) The tendency toward work, a right of the person who suffers from unemployment. From the nature of work one can deduce the fundamental rights about salary, the relationship between work and capital, etc.

*e)* The inclination toward a political society and the various forms of association, knowledge of which brings us to questions about forms of government, the legitimacy of authority, the right of association and many other things besides.

*f)* The tendency toward communication; issuing from its purpose is the obligation to truthfulness, the right of a good reputation, etc.

*g)* Finally, the inclination toward knowledge and the different forms of culture and art, from which flow the right to be educated, the freedom of instruction and other rights and obligations.

## 4.   Normative character of human nature

We can clearly ask why human nature is normative and the nature of other beings is not. In effect, it may seem that what is reasonable is to treat each thing according to its nature: it does not seem reasonable to sail with an automobile or to use a Formula 1 car for ploughing fields. Would it not be reasonable to treat human beings (or for them to act) according to their nature just as it is reasonable to treat things and animals in this manner?

I do not know if the reader has had the occasion to deal with mules. I have done so because of the military service which I completed in the last year of my studies. I ended up in a gathering of recruits at the command of the captain who wanted to show that he could make some good muleteers out of lawyers (meaning those with law degrees); aside from this he was a man of excellent qualities. And he made me the driver of a mule called Romo. Here I learned that treating mules with too much indulgence is to make them useless, but excessive roughness makes them suspicious, wild, unmanageable and inclined to kick and be demanding. Without a doubt, knowing how to treat animals is an art, which is what we were acknowledging when we applauded the horse-trainer in the ring used for performing these exercises and difficult tricks. All of this, though, is not natural law. In each case, this is an art which consists of knowing how to obtain the usefulness that is desired.

For my part, I succeeded in coming to understand Romo and make him offer the service which the Army sought from him. I did not hereby fulfill any precept of the natural law regarding mules; I was simply not a bad soldier (I also did not get any further); I used a technique. When we say that it is reasonable to use things or to treat animals according to their nature, we are not alluding to the moral law but to a technique, an art—and it would be logical for Seneca to pardon me or be confused about this since he was a Stoic. I do not know what happened to Romo when they gave me other appointments after the oath to the flag. Hypothetically speaking, what is clear is that he could be sold to a food mill for animals to be sacrificed and canned; one could obtain soap from his fat, or they could make drums from his hide, as happened to the donkey in the fable of Samaniego.[10]

This, among other things, cannot be done with humans. In the technical sense of the expression "being able to do," it is clear that, except for making drums with his hide, it and other things can be done. Nevertheless, *it cannot be done* in the moral sense of the word (it must not be done). And this *is not disputable*; it is not a *point of view*. Or might the reader think that he cannot be transformed into dog food, so fashionable nowadays simply because the majority of people opine that it would have a bad taste? It is certainly not disputable; it is *natural law*.

Acting according to nature or being treated in conformity with it is something more than a technique for human beings. It is a demand of their nature, which requires that the behaviour which leads humans to follow their natural ends is *obligatory*, and contrary behaviour is prohibited. We have already stated what the foundation of this is: the rational, personal nature of humans. Since humans are persons, their dignity, which derives from their being and their ends, demands that they act and be

---

10. Translator's note: Félix María Samaniego was an 18th century Spanish fabulist, among whose writings was *El asno y el cochino* [The Donkey and the Pig]. The donkey found himself envying the pig, whose life was one of leisure and plenty, while the donkey's was one of labor and struggle. In the end, he realised how unenviable the life of the pig was since it ended in slaughter.

treated in certain specific ways. These rules constitute the natural law, which has the character of true law.

## 5.  Function of natural law

Human nature is free; it possesses freedom. Therefore, natural law supposes that humans have the faculty to govern themselves, which is one of the aspects of this freedom. Consequently, natural law does not encompass all activity possible for humans or the whole realm of laws. Since natural law is a law of and for freedom, it empowers humans and society to issue laws: *positive laws* or those posited by humans. What then is the function of natural law? Its specific function consists of being the *basis* or *foundation* of the juridical system and the political order. What a constitution represents in a system of positive laws—the basis of the legal system, the inspiring criterion and the criterion of validity—so is natural law with respect to every system of laws.

Positive laws adjust themselves to natural law as their basis or foundation; they derive from it. Since persons by nature have a right to health, positive laws build up the whole legal health system and the system of social security. The reason is very simple, and we have spoken of it more than once: every human cultural thing derives from a natural datum. Thus can we see the inspiring character of natural law with respect to positive law; if positive laws derive from a nucleus of natural law, they are obliged (it is their mission) to order the social reality in accord with this nucleus: in order to be founded on the right to life and health, the legal health system cannot be organised as a criminal system designed to kill or injure persons. This would not make sense (and so neither do laws legalising abortion and euthanasia). At the same time, the limiting character (a criterion of validity) that natural law possesses can be seen. We said earlier that there are things which human beings are not *able* to do in the moral order, even though they are technically capable of doing them. And so, humans *cannot* issue immoral or unjust laws. If by "to be able" is understood the ability to write an immoral or unjust "law," to discuss it in Parliament, to promulgate it and to order compliance with it immediately by means of the police, such a thing undoubtedly can be done. This power, though, is a fact, a system of coercion; it is not the law which *obliges* a person to obedience in virtue of legal justice. Properly speaking, it is a false law, just as tinsel is not gold or counterfeit money is not true money. Such an immoral or unjust "law" is not a true law which morally binds a person; it does not correspond to human moral reality but to the sad class of coercion and institutional violence.

Positivists are usually shocked at the fact that natural law is a criterion for the validity of positive laws. Were it so, they say, the legal system would be undermined, which would create juridical instability and an unknown number of more catastrophes. This attitude is highly akin to the shock of the Pharisees; in fact, they cannot actually believe what they say in seriousness. In the first place, it is obvious that, in a juridical system so evolved as ours, it is for judges to analyse and determine a possible contrast between natural law and positive law; and as is seen in the sources, the Roman jurists and the judges with them used this rule, and not only did it not crush Roman law but it remained an exemplary juridical system of great perfection. In the second place, judges now do this (in part) using other expressions—values or general principles of law, human rights, etc.—and nothing evil is happening; rather, better justice is being obtained. In the third place, this same technique is followed with constitutional law; and no catastrophe occurs, but the contrary.

Moreover, there is a juridical system—the canonical system—in which thousands of judges and hundreds of jurists constantly apply natural law as an informing principle and a criterion of the validity of positive laws; and not only have they not brought about the collapse of the system, but it is exemplary in more than one aspect. Jurists devoted to secular law (we are not speaking specifically of Spaniards) have already desired to obtain a matrimonial system as perfect as the canonical one, in place of the indigestible collages which they usually offer us when we assist with judicial sentences, which seem to have entirely lost a minimally reasonable notion of what marriage is. (Up to now I do not know of any Spaniard of this kind.)

## 6.   Who states what natural law is?

In the years which I have spent explaining natural
law, I have never been wanting for a student in the
first days of the course to stand up and ask this question: "And *who says* what is natural law or what is a
natural right?" It is a question which my interlocu-
tors invariably formulate, both in private conversations and in the conversations which follow talks
and conferences on these themes. I confess that this
question always occurs to me as so very precipi-
tated. Who says what the laws of biology are?
Biologists. Who says what the laws of economics
are? Economists. Who *says* what the law is? Jurists;
this is their science and their function, as we said at
the beginning. Who *says* what natural law is?
Regarding what both positive and natural law are,
the Roman jurists, the medieval jurists, and modern
jurists declared it, and contemporary jurists declare
it (excluding positivists). Just as with positive law, it
is for jurists to articulate the natural law in two ways:
1) with the public juridical authority of judges, binding for each concrete case, and 2) with the private
authority of jurists, experts in natural law. This is
what the duty and social function of jurists consists
of: to declare and to classify law, whether natural or
positive.

And who says what natural law is? The response
is easy in light of what we have said. Declaring the
distinct aspects of natural law belongs to moralists,
jurists, and experts in political science. So it has

always been in history. The Stoics wrote splendid pages in this regard, as did Plato and Cicero; and moralists for their part, especially theologians, have written whole libraries. Why is it that disparate criteria, disputable points and errors are at times observed in them? (For example, slavery seemed natural to Aristotle, while the Sophists, the Stoics and the Roman jurists—the most correct on this point— judged it to be an institution positively contrary to natural freedom.) Well, do not physicians, biologists, astronomers, physicists and many others at times disagree? Hence, will we say that the human body, the laws of biology, or heavenly bodies do not exist? What does the existence of a reality have to do with uncertainties of human knowledge about it?

Astronomy, a *precise science* as they say, seems very respectable to all of us, and we take much notice of it—not from proven conclusions but from hypotheses coming from the work of astronomers. Well, never in the field of natural law has there been a fiasco so plain and so capable of discrediting a science as has happened with astronomy. Have astronomers not asserted throughout the ages that the sun revolves around the earth, and it turned out that precisely the contrary is the truth? Nevertheless, when astronomy observed its error, within the first moment of disagreement, everyone rejoiced and praised the capacity of the human mind to discover the truth, in spite of the fact that appearances can at first lead us to error; when the fiasco was discovered, astronomy was strengthened. When errors or discrepancies are observed among experts in natural law, in virtue of what rule do some comment loudly that, on the one hand, natural law does not exist because of this, while, on the other hand, they do not say that the sun and the earth do not exist, or that the laws which govern the motion of the stars do not exist in view of the colossal error of the astronomers? Aristotle thought that slavery was based on natural law, and was he mistaken; but of course, was Aristotle infallible? Let us be reasonable: do we not know that Aristotle was mistaken because we understand that the state of freedom is from natural law (as the Sophists already stated before Aristotle)? Therefore, we can know natural law with certainty; otherwise, we could not know that Aristotle was mistaken.

We should compare what was said by Aristotle, Plato, Marcus Aurelius and Cicero, by the Wisdom books of the Bible, and in the writings of the Holy Fathers, Saint Thomas Aquinas, Averroes, Maimonides, Gotius, Pufendorf, Saint Alfonso Maria Liguori, and the modern and contemporary moralists—with the exception of the anti-morality of existentialists, analytics and structuralists. Besides discrepancies on *some* concrete points, we will observe substantial agreement. Are there any experimental sciences—which we virtually adore as new divinities and whose experts we hold as oracles who are all but infallible—which can present substantial agreement for so long a time and in so extensive a subject matter? Indeed, the objections made against natural law in this manner are usually the fruit of an admitted lack of seriousness.

Who states what natural law is? Those who understand it: moralists, jurists, and political thinkers. Nevertheless, holding primacy among them are the moralists for the reasons pointed out earlier; while the juridical and political sciences only study one aspect of natural law, the moralist studies it in its entirety: therefore, his science is qualified to understand it in a better and more complete manner.

The reader will undoubtedly not fail to recognise that, since natural law and divine law come from God, the Author of nature, there is a higher wisdom than that which I just brought into focus: divine revelation interpreted by the Church. If we rely on divine revelation, those who declare what natural law is are the organs of the solemn ecclesiastical Magisterium: the Pope and the Ecumenical Council, when they define a proposition of natural law (and they declare it unfailingly). Without the intention of defining propositions of natural law in a definitive manner, the ecclesiastical Magisterium—the Pope and the Bishops—often declares what is from natural law in light of revelation; here its teachings receive the name "ordinary Magisterium."

## 7.   Knowledge of natural law

In light of what we just explained, does this mean that only experts and specialists know about natural law? Undoubtedly not. All of us humans have sufficient knowledge of ourselves and our environment, which equips us for living normally. When we say that Newton described the law of gravity, we do not mean that beyond him no one would have been informed about the fact that bodies have weight and fall; the entire world knows this. What Newton described was the reason why bodies fall: attraction to the earth; others could know that bodies fall, even if they might have explained it in another way. It is like with that sergeant that I had (a great person) when I was a recruit who, after giving us a day of theoretical class, explained to us that bodies fall by the force of gravity; after he said that, I remained silent a moment and added, as if speaking to myself, "Even if there were no gravity, things of all kinds would fall by their own weight."

Every human being has a general or common knowledge of the fundamental and basic dictates of natural law; he knows that it is evil to kill an innocent person, or to steal from or extort someone. If he is asked *why this is so*, he will probably shy away from people, and he may not know what to say except, "just because it is evil." Natural law is a dictate of reason; and in the understanding of reason, two successive and connected moments can be distinguished. There is a common or general exercise or use of reason, which is proper to every person who has reached the normal development of this faculty. Then there is a second moment following the previous which investigates and comprehends the why and the how and deepens one's learning:

this is *scientific knowledge*. With respect to natural law as well, there is common knowledge and scientific knowledge. Common knowledge is that which enables humans to live in harmony with natural law, except on specific, more difficult or obscure points, which are accessible only to experts: to the moralist or the jurist. In such cases, one must consult an expert, as happens in the other ordinary areas of life.

This is a cause of surprise to some. Is not the natural law engraved on the person's heart? Why then are there precepts which require consultation? This surprise comes from inadequately interpreting what it means to say that humans have natural law engraved in their being. There are those who think that this means that persons are born with all the precepts of natural law written in their reason and in their brain, something like a computer that might carry an installed programme from the factory; it would be enough to touch it or the appropriate buttons, and the precepts of natural law would appear on the screen or on the printer. This is an error. With respect to the natural law (and this is sufficient for saying that the law is inscribed in him), the person is born only with a *correct disposition* of reason (the innate habit or virtue of synderesis) by which it is infallibly understood that the good must be done and evil avoided, even if he or she as a free being ultimately might not act accordingly. Likewise, one is born with natural inclinations which one perceives as forces ordering him toward his natural ends. He knows, then, that it is good to act in conformity with these inclinations—therefore, one *must* do it or one *can* do it, according to the type of inclination one is dealing with—and it is evil to deviate from one's ends. In this way, one knows that one must take care of one's life and health, that homicide is a crime, that being married is a good and a right of every person, that one must work and that laziness is a vice, that political society belongs to human nature, etc.

As can be seen, knowledge of natural law is not innate in the sense of having a list of the precepts of natural law impressed in our reason from the moment we are conceived in our mother's womb. Synderesis and natural inclinations are innate; the easy and safe knowledge of the fundamental precepts of natural law derives from this. In every case, though, the precepts of natural law are a work of reason, which does not err with regard to the cited fundamental principles. Since human reason is not infallible, knowing the precepts which derive from these fundamental precepts can become difficult, and erring in the process of reason in order to know them can be easy. Hence, it is not surprising to discover that Aristotle himself was mistaken in a precept of natural law or that there are disputed points among moralists and among jurists. There is nothing special or rare about this if one realises how human reasons knows; the contrary would be rare. Without a doubt, what we have just said—and what we will say next in this regard—requires much elaboration, but now is not the moment for this (these points are treated in any good manual of morality or natural law); but let us continue the discussion.

## 8.   "Forgetting" natural law

Some are also at times surprised by the fact that, in different eras (and the current one is an example of this), there are precepts of the natural law that are not observed by many people. Here, too, there is an error in perspective. Natural law is the law of the person's moral reality, that is, of the realm of the persons' free activity; therefore, natural law can be disobeyed, even though one ought not to do so. If it could not be disobeyed, it would be an instinct or a physical law, not a law of human moral reality. The fact that there are many who disobey *some* precepts of natural law only means that human depravity is very extensive. (It is impossible that all or a majority of them would be disobeyed since this would lead to the disappearance of humans; e.g., all would have committed suicide had they not first been assassinated.) In a manner of speaking, this is the risk of freedom, which has nothing to do with the existence of freedom—that is, it is a law of freedom, and consequently it is a law which it is possible in fact for the human person to disobey.

The cause of surprise for others is not so much the fact that many people disobey some precepts of natural law, but the fact that those who have been accustomed to disobey it end up forgetting it and even defend what they do. On this point, one should be a good psychologist and know how precisely to distinguish what is behind such defences or forgetful attitudes. We human beings forget the precepts of natural law less easily than it seems. Not long ago, a famous, excellent actress died, whose emotional life was in certain aspects not exemplary. When she was criticised, she, on the one hand, defended herself by saying that people do not have the right to interfere in the private life of others; on the other hand, she confessed that she did not understand why people believed that she was an immaculate woman; she was like other persons, and, she concluded, all human beings are partially good and partially evil. And so she was aware that there was something evil in her behaviour.

We human beings often construct a mountain of reasons for justifying our actions which are contrary to natural law. This does not mean, though, that we are unaware that we do evil; it only means that *we prefer* what is contrary to natural law, and we find some aspect of the good in it—since synderesis is innate, and consequently we only act for some reason related to the good. Not long before the time of the famous actress to whom I alluded, a no less famous actor died. In some statements made a few months before his death, this actor related that, throughout his career, he had tripped up a number of people who could have surpassed him. He recognised that he had done wrong, but he added that, despite being wrong, if he could be born again and find himself in the same circumstances, he would do

the same thing. In such cases there is not a forgetfulness of natural law if one recognises that he does
what is evil. What happens is that a person commits
himself to egoism and prefers non-compliance with
natural law. Can natural law be forgotten?
Not at all; it is rather that there is a preference for
behaviour opposed to it, drowsiness of the conscience, and things of this sort. There can be social
environments in which acting contrary to some
aspect of natural law may be a social behavioural
standard that is praised and *required* if one does not
want to be rejected. If we consider these cases,
though, we will frequently reach the conclusion that
they, too, do not entail a true forgetfulness of natural
law; rather, they entail a gradual confusion of reason
and conscience. This does not remove responsibility
for the moral guilt which arises, even if such guilt is
somewhat mitigated by the ideological or environ-
mental manipulation of the matter at issue.

Still, there can certainly be some cases in which
it is appropriate to speak of a *forgetfulness* of natural
law which is not accompanied by moral turpitude.
Such cases never refer to the primary or fundamental precepts but to the precepts which suppose a
fuller, more perfect knowledge of human nature. In
other words, beyond the scope of the fundamental
precepts, the phenomena of ignorance and error can
occur. The explanation is quite simple: precepts of
natural law are not judgements that are innate to reason but judgements that are obtained by the process
of reasoning—certainly elementary and almost

immediate. And consequently, there can be mistakes in this process of reasoning, either because of an insufficient knowledge of human nature or through fault of the passions or vices which negatively influence the correct functioning of reason. Human reason makes mistakes, although they may be rectifiable by study and, with respect to natural law above all, by rectitude of the will.

## 9.  Universality of natural law

Every human being is born with the rectitude of reason (synderesis) necessary for knowing infallibly the primary principles of natural law: do good, and avoid evil. By nature, human beings likewise have inclinations which are proper to them: preservation of their being, the tendencies toward association, knowledge and communication. Also, their being and their ends have the same demand. Hence, natural law is universal.

It is certain that each person has his individual characteristics; we are all different. At the same time, though, it is no less certain that we all have a common substratum or base; we have all been made according to the same schema, if I may be permitted the expression. Differences, therefore, are accidental and secondary. If we observe the body, all of us human beings follow the same plan: the same bones, the same tissues, the same organs, the same senses, etc. Likewise, we all have a soul and body, identical spiritual faculties (reason and will), etc. We all have the same inclinations; we are all equally persons; and we all possess the same value and dignity. In conclusion, we all have the same *nature*, the same *ends*, and the same *obligations* with respect to how we behave and how we are treated. Natural law is equal and the same for all human beings and for all peoples.

What may vary is the precept or precepts which individual persons or a social environment *violate* with greater frequency. Some steal, others are idle, others lie, etc. Human beings and peoples have dominant vices. This is not an indication that undermines the universality of natural law; rather it is proof of the universality of original sin. Also, human beings and peoples have their preferences with respect to vices.

In this regard, it seems profitable to return to something that we already explained earlier. Some are scandalised by the fact that some people appear to have a dominant vice; it seems to them that natural law is not universal. (For example, according to reports, some nomads of the African deserts usually concentrate on robbing their neighbour, some peoples have been cannibals, Western civilisation suffers from violence and terrorism, and white South Africans have practiced racial discrimination; we could do this for each and every people.) Their process of reasoning is mistaken: there is a confusion of natural law with physical law. If natural law were a physical law, no one would violate it; and so, all human beings are hungry, sleepy, have a heartbeat, etc. However, since natural law is *moral* (a law of freedom) and not physical, the human person is capable of not complying with it; and given the existence of moral evil and the inclination toward evil, we do not comply with its precepts. That being said, this does not prove that natural law is not universal; rather, it proves that original sin is universal.

The fact is, upon reaching this point, I find myself very perplexed. It seems that I was saying how appropriate it is in this introduction to speak about natural law, and still I have not mentioned the deeds of Sophocles in making Antigone the protagonist or the famous words which he put in her mouth; but now is not the time to describe these. In no way should the reader feel that he has been cheated; he can read the original, which is always better, and, if he is a student of law, he will certainly not be freed of the inevitable citation of Sophocles and his *Antigone*: it will come.

# Chapter X

# Canon Law

At the origins of the modern juridical science we find not only *lawyers*—who owe their beginning to a famous, sparingly-known teacher named Irnerius, with the precedent of one Peppo of whom scarcely more than the name is known—but also *canonists*, with the figure of the also too-little known Master Gratian. Up to now, it has been considered indisputable that precedence belonged to lawyers, whose methods were followed by canonists. Nevertheless, more recent investigations about the work of Gratian have called this precedence into question; at the moment, this is based on the opposition of medieval Romanists. In any case, beyond the juridical regime of States and their relationships with the Catholic Church (the regime of *Christendom*), in its origins, the modern juridical science is indebted as much to lawyers as to canonists in the creation of the system of *utrumque ius*, two laws: the *ius civile* (civil law) and the *ius canonicum* (canon law), which governed the juridical life of Europe for ages.

With the arrival of the Protestant Reformation, this system disappeared in order to enclose canon law within the limits of the Catholic Church. However, although it was separated from secular law, canon law continued to live, and canonists find themselves within an important sector of the juridical science, with their faculties of canon law and their intense scientific activity and practice. On the other hand, it must not be forgotten that canon law governs subject matters that are very relevant to everyone's life, such as marriage, and it does so within an independent and sovereign community containing millions of faithful who surpass the most inhabited and vast States in number, with great diversity. No State laws have the binding scope that canon law has, even taking into account the law governing the union of States such as the European Union. We are dealing, then, with a juridical phenomenon which no jurist can neglect, and one must necessarily make reference to it in an introduction to law, at least summarily.

Canon law is clearly distinguished from secular law (the law of political communities) by the matters which it treats; for these laws pertain to societies of a distinct nature. They only converge on the topic of marriage, over which the Church claims jurisdiction for herself when it is between the baptised, employing a canonical marriage system much more complete than civil marriage systems.

These undeniable differences in content between canon law and secular law must not cause a misunderstanding about the genuine nature of canon law. In the Church, there are true relationships of commutative justice (e.g., contracts), distributive justice (e.g., the faithful have a right to the sacraments), and legal justice (in the Church there is authentic legislative power as well as judicial and executive governance); it includes penal law, a judicial system, etc.

If true justice exists, true *ius* exists, as (we hope) has been sufficiently clear in the previous pages.

For this reason, in line with a glorious tradition which is traced back to the beginnings of the European juridical science, to be a canonist is to be a jurist; the canonical science is an important (as well as original) sector of the juridical science, and the method it follows is a juridical method.

What is this method, though? The question is not empty since, during the 20th century, save for very few exceptions, the majority of canonical activity has been declining and marked by meagre progression: it is a faithful follower of the exegetical method of legal texts, a method already surpassed by the secular juridical science, which on the whole has seen brilliant eras; and after the School of Exegesis following the Napoleonic Code, the 19th century had already abandoned the exegetical method by substituting it with the systematic method. Only some minority groups have been spared this decline, groups known as the Italian School and the School of Lombardía.

In the last 25 years of the 20th century, while the majority of canonical activity has continued without moving beyond exegesis, canonists following the systematic method have already emerged with treatises and manuals which in no way have to be envious of the quality and juridical standards found in the secular juridical science. Therefore, a rebirth of canonical research is being prompted, and this will undoubtedly bear its fruit in the 21st century.

# Bibliography

As a possible broadening of the themes treated in this introduction, we indicate here some books that can be consulted.[11]

APARISI, Á., *Ética y deontología para juristas* (Pamplona: EUNSA, 2006).

ARISTOTLE, *Ética a Nicómaco* (Madrid: Centro de Estudios Constitucionales, 1981); *Nicomachean Ethics*, Penguin Classics, Hugh TREDENNICK (ed.) (London: The Penguin Group, 2004).

BALLESTEROS, J., *Sobre el sentido del Derecho*, 3rd ed. (Madrid: Tecnos, 2001).

BURKE, C., *Conciencia y libertad* (Madrid: Rialp, 1976); *Conscience and Freedom*, 2nd ed. (Makati City: Sinagala, 1992).

CASTAN, J., *Los derechos del hombre* (Madrid: Reus, 1976).

d'ENTREVES, A.P., *Derecho Natural* (Madrid: Aguilar, 1972); *Natural Law. An Introduction to Legal Philosophy* (London: Hutchison's Library, 1957).

d'ORS, A., *Una introducción al estudio del Derecho* (Madrid: Rialp, 1982). This book is very original and evocative.

DE CASTRO CID, B., *Manual de Teoría del Derecho*, 3rd ed. (Madrid: Ed. Universitarias, 2007).

FINNIS, J. M., *Ley natural y derechos naturales* (Buenos Aires: Abeledo-Perrot, 2000); *Natural Law and Natural Rights*, Clarendon Law Series, 9th ed. (Oxford: Oxford University Press, 1997).

---

11. Translator's note: In addition to the citations provided by the author, we refer the reader to original English editions or translations, to original French editions of the cited texts where available, as well as to a few other English titles.

FRIEDRICH, C.J., *La Filosofía del Derecho* (México: Fondo de Cultura Económica, 1964).

FUENMAYOR, A. DE, *Divorcio: legalidad, moralidad y cambio social* (Pamplona: EUNSA, 1981).

GALLEGO, E., *Fundamentos para una Teoría del Derecho*, 2nd ed. (Madrid: Dykinson, 2006).

GUITTON, J., *El trabajo intelectual* (Madrid: Rialp, 1977); *Le travail intellectuel* (Paris: Flammarion, 1994).

HERNÁNDEZ GIL, A., *El abogado y el razonamiento jurídico* (Madrid: Sucesores de Rivadeneyra, 1975).

———, *Metodología de la Ciencia del Derecho* (Madrid: Tecnos, 1971).

HERVADA, J., *Introducción crítica al Derecho Natural*, 10th ed. (Pamplona: EUNSA, 2001); *Critical Introduction to Natural Law*, Gratianus Series (Montréal: Wilson & Lafleur Ltée, 2006).

———, *Lecciones propedéuticas de Filosofía del Derecho*, 4th ed. (Pamplona: EUNSA, 2008).

IHERING, R., *Bromas y veras en la jurisprudencia* (Buenos Aires: Ed. Juridicas, 1974).

MACINTYRE, A., *Tras la virtud* (Barcelona: Grijalbo, 1987); *After Virtue*, 3rd ed. (Notre Dame: University of Notre Dame Press, 2007).

———, *Justicia y racionalidad*, 2nd ed. (Madrid: Ediciones Internacionales Universitarias, 2001); *Whose Justice? Which Rationality?* (Notre Dame: University of Notre Dame Press, 1988).

MARTÍNEZ DORAL, J.M., *La estructura del conocimiento jurídico* (Pamplona: EUNSA, 1963).

MELINA, L., *Sharing in Christ's Virtues: For a Renewal of Moral Theology in Light of* Veritatis splendor, W. E. MAY (trans.) (Washington, D.C.: CUA Press, 2001).

MILLÁN PUELLES, A., *Persona humana y justicia social* (Madrid: Rialp, 1982).

OLLERO, A., *El derecho en teoría* (Cizur Menor: Aranzadi, 2007).

PÉREZ LUÑO, A. *Teoría del Derecho*, 6th ed. (Madrid: Tecnos, 2007).

PIEPER, J., *Las virtudes fundamentales* (Madrid: Rialp, 1976); *The Four Cardinal Virtues* (Notre Dame: The University of Notre Dame Press, 1956). See *Justice*, L. E. LYNCH (trans.) (New York: Pantheon Books, 1955), which is an excellent treatise on justice.

———, *El ocio y la vida intelectual* (Madrid: Rialp, 1962); *Leisure. The Basis of Culture*, G. MALSBARY (trans.) (Chicago: St. Augustine's Press, 1998).

PLATO, *La República* (Madrid: Centro de Estudios Constitucionales, 1969); *The Republic*, 2nd ed., A. BLOOM (trans.) (New York: Basic Books, 1991).

PRECIADO HERNÁNDEZ, R., *Lecciones de Filosofía del Derecho* (México: Editorial Ius, 1960).

RECASENS SICHES, *Panorama del pensamiento jurídico en el siglo XX* (Méjico: Porrua, 1963).

ROBLES, G., *Introducción a la Teoría del Derecho* (Madrid: Debate, 2003).

SCHOUPPE, J.-P., *Le réalisme juridique* (Bruxelles: E. Story-Scientia, 1987).

TRUYOL, A., *Los derechos humanos* (Madrid: Tecnos, 1968).

VARA, J., *Libres, buenos y justos: como miembros del mismo cuerpo. Lecciones de Teoría del Derecho y del Derecho Natural* (Madrid: Tecnos, 2007).

VILLEY, M., *Compendio de Filosofía del Derecho*, 2 vols., Spanish edition (Pamplona: EUNSA, 1979 and 1981); *Philosophie du droit* (Paris: Dalloz, 2001).

VON HILDEBRAND, D., *Ethics* (Quincy: Franciscan Herald Press, 1953).

———, *Fundamental Moral Attitudes* (New York: Longmans, Green and Co., 1950).

**Last published / Dernières publications**

### HANDBOOKS / MANUELS

*What is Law? The Modern Response of Juridical Realism. An Introduction to Law.*
Javier HERVADA. Translated by William L. Daniel, 2009, ISBN 978-2-89127-910-9.

*The Pastoral Companion. A Canon Law Handbook for Catholic Ministry*, Fourth updated edition, John M. HUELS, 2009, ISBN 978-2-89127-891-1.

### MONOGRAPHS / MONOGRAPHIES

*Les archives ecclésiales, diocésaines et paroissiales.* Patrimoine archivistique de l'Église catholique, Assemblée des chanceliers et chancelières du Québec,2009, ISBN 978-2-89127-917-8.

*The Seal of Confession and Canadian Law*, Gregory J. ZUBACZ, 2009, ISBN 978-2-89127-888-1.

### PROCEEDINGS / ACTES

*Études sur la prélature de l'Opus Dei* dans le cadre du vingt-cinquième anniversaire de la constitution apostolique *Ut Sit*, traduction de l'italien et édition par Jean-Pierre Schouppe, 2009, ISBN 978-2-89127-889-8.

*Studies on the Prelature of Opus Dei* on the Twenty-Fifth Anniversary of the Apostolic Constitution *Ut sit*. Translated and Edited by Paul HAYWARD, 2009, ISBN 978-2-89127-887-4.

**Forthcoming / En préparation**

### HANDBOOKS / MANUELS

*Justice in the Church. A Fundamental Theory of Canon Law.* Carlos José ERRÁZURIZ M., English translation by Jean Gray in collaboration with Michael Dunnigan. ISBN 978-2-89127-910-9.

*L'organisation du gouvernement de l'Église*, J.I. ARRIETA, ISBN 978-2-89127-876-8.

*Les clés du Code*, A. BUNGE, ISBN 978-2-89127-843-0.

### RESEARCH TOOLS / INSTRUMENTS DE RECHERCHE

Ministerium Iustitiæ. *Jurisprudence of the Supreme Tribunal of the Apostolic Signatura.* (Official Latin with English Translation), William DANIEL, compilator, ISBN 978-2-89127-890-4.

**Published in 2008 / Parus en 2008**

### PROCEEDINGS / ACTES

*Procédure pénale et la protection des droits dans la législation canonique*, P. M. DUGAN, 2008, ISBN 978-2-89127-849-2.

### HANDBOOKS / MANUELS

*Comprendre les Écritures*, S. HAHN, 2008, ISBN 978-2-89127-845-4.

*Droit canonique des biens*, J.-P. SCHOUPPE, 2008, ISBN 978-2-89127-856-0.

*Associations of Christ's Faithful*, L. Cardinal MARTÍNEZ SISTACH, 2008, ISBN 978-2-89127-848-5.

### NOTEBOOKS / CAHIERS

*Christ's Faithful in the World. The Secular Character of the Laity*, J. MIRAS, 2008, ISBN 978-2-89127-870-6.

#### Other published / Déjà parus

*Introduction to the History of the Sources of Canon Law I — The Ancient Law up to the Decretum of Gratian*, Brian E. FERME, 2007, ISBN 978-2-89127-805-8.

*Introduction to the Study of Canon Law*, J. HERVADA, 2007, ISBN 978-2-89127-836-2.

*A Handbook on Canon Law*, 2nd updated edition, J. T. MARTÍN DE AGAR, 2007, ISBN 978-2-89127-804-1.

*Liturgie et droit — Le droit liturgique dans le système du droit canonique de l'Église catholique*, John HUELS, traduit par Jean PELLETIER, 2007, ISBN 978-2-89127-811-9.

*Fidèles dans le monde. La sécularité des laïcs chrétiens*, Jorge MIRAS, 2007, ISBN 978-2-89127-841-6.

*The Juridical Mind of Saint Josemaria Escriva A Brief History of the Canonical Path of Opus Dei*, 2nd updated edition, E. CAPARROS, 2007, ISBN 978-2-89127-833-1.

*La mentalité juridique de saint Josémaria Escriva. Un bref historique de l'itinéraire canonique de l'Opus Dei*, E. CAPARROS, 2007, ISBN 9778-2-89127-834-8.

*Dictionnaire biographique des cardinaux du XIXᵉ siècle*, Jean LEBLANC, 2007, ISBN 978-2-89127-801-0.

*Code de droit canonique bilingue et annoté* (3ᵉ éd.), E. CAPARROS, H. AUBÉ (directeurs), 2007, ISBN 978-2-89127-768-6.

*Symposium on Dignitas connubii*, Patricia M. DUGAN & Luis NAVARRO (Editors), 2006, 2nd printing: April 2009, ISBN 2-89127-782-1.

*Canonical and Pastoral Guide for Parishes, Canadian Edition*, Assembly of Catholic Bishops of Québec, J. PELLETIER (Editor), 2006, ISBN 2-89127-779-1.

*Guide canonique et pastoral au service des paroisses. Édition canadienne*, Assemblée des évêques catholiques du Québec, J. PELLETIER (directeur), 2006, ISBN 2-89127-778-3.

*A Critical Introduction to Natural Law*, J. HERVADA, 2006, 2nd printing: April 2009, ISBN 2-89127-776-7.

*Advocacy Vademecum*, Patricia M. DUGAN (Editor), 2006, ISBN 2-89127-777-5.

*Liturgy and Law — Liturgical Law in the System of Roman Catholic Canon Law*, J. M. HUELS, 2006, ISBN 2-89127-773-2.

*Canonical and Pastoral Guide for Parishes*, Assembly of Bishops of Québec, J. PELLETIER (Editor), 2005, ISBN 2-89127-640-X.

*Incrementa in Progressu 1983 Codicis Iuris Canonici with a Multilingual Introduction (English, Français, Italiano, Español, Deutsch, Polski)*, E. N. PETERS, 2005, ISBN 2-89127-663-7.

*The Penal Process and the Protection of Rights in Canon Law*, Patricia M. DUGAN (Editor), 2005, ISBN 2-89127-664-7.

*Code of Canon Law Annotated*, 2nd revised and updated edition, E. CAPARROS, H. AUBÉ (Editors), 2004, International edition, MTF ISBN 1-890177-44-X/Canadian edition W&L, ISBN 2-89127-629-9.

*Exegetical Commentary on the Code of Canon Law*, Á. MARZOA, J. MIRAS, R. RODRÍGUEZ-OCAÑA (Editors), E. CAPARROS (General Editor, English edition).

International edition 2004:
- Volume I Chicago, MTF ISBN 1-890177-34-2/Montréal, W&L, ISBN 2-89127-621-3.
- Volume II/1 Chicago, MTF ISBN 1-890177-35-0/Montréal, W&L, ISBN 2-89127-622-1.
- Volume II/2 Chicago, MTF ISBN 1-890177-36-9/Montréal, W&L, ISBN 2-89127-623-X.
- Volume III/1 Chicago, MTF ISBN 1-890177-37-7/Montréal, W&L, ISBN 2-89127-624-8.
- Volume III/2 Chicago, MTF ISBN 1-890177-38-5/Montréal, W&L, ISBN 2-89127-625-6.
- Volume IV/1 Chicago, MTF ISBN 1-890177-39-3/Montréal, W&L, ISBN 2-89127-626-4.
- Volume IV/2 Chicago, MTF ISBN 1-890177-40-7/Montréal, W&L, ISBN 2-89127-627-2.
- Volume V Chicago, MTF ISBN 1-890177-41-5/Montréal, W&L, ISBN 2-89127-628-0.

*Guide canonique et pastoral au service des paroisses II*, Assemblée des évêques du Québec, J. PELLETIER (directeur), 2004, ISBN 2-89127-639-6.

*Dictionnaire biographique des évêques catholiques du Canada (1658-2002)*, J. LEBLANC, 2002, ISBN 2-89127-506-8.

*Governance Structures Within the Catholic Church*, J.I. ARRIETA, 2000, 2nd printing: April 2009, ISBN 2-89127-518-7.

*Tabulæ congruentiæ inter Codicem iuris canonici et versiones anteriores canonum: With a Multilingual Introduction (English, Français, Italiano, Español, Deutsch)*, E. N. PETERS, 2000, ISBN 2-89127-500-4.

*A Handbook on Canon Law*, J. T. MARTÍN DE AGAR, 1999, ISBN 2-89127-457-1.

*Code de droit canonique bilingue et annoté*, (2ᵉ éd.), E. CAPARROS, M. THÉRIAULT, J. THORN (†) (directeurs), 1999, 2ᵉ tirage 2003, ISBN 2-89127-460-1.

*La charge pastorale d'une paroisse sans curé*, B. A. CUSAK & T. G. SULLIVAN, trad. et adaptation par M. THÉRIAULT, 1997, ISBN 2-89127-417-2.

*NCCB/Conférence des évêques catholiques des États-Unis. Le manuel de l'évêque*, trad. par M. THÉRIAULT, 1994, ISBN 2-89127-309-5 (épuisé).

*Code of Canon Law Annotated*, E. CAPARROS, M. THÉRIAULT, J. THORN (Editors), 1st edition: March 1993, 2nd printing: October 1993, 3rd printing: 1996, 4th printing: 1997, 5th printing: 2000, ISBN 2-89127-232-3 (out of print).

*Code de droit canonique*, E. CAPARROS, M. THÉRIAULT, J. THORN (†) (directeurs), édition bilingue et annotée, 1ʳᵉ édition : mars 1990, 2ᵉ tirage : décembre 1990, 3ᵉ tirage : 1994, 4ᵉ tirage : 1995, ISBN 2-89127-153-X (épuisé).

Orders to / Commander à :

| WILSON & LAFLEUR LTÉE

40, Notre-Dame Est
Montréal (Québec) Canada H2Y 1B9
Tél. : 514 875-6326 / 1 800 363-2327
Téléc. : 514 875-8356
www.wilsonlafleur.com

| USA

www.CanonLawBooks.com
2662 East Allegheny Avenue
Philadelphia, PA 19134-5115
Phone: 215 634-2355 • Fax: 215 634-2373

| EUROPE

**Éditions Le Laurier**
19, passage Jean Nicot
75007 PARIS
Tél. : +33 1.45.51.55.08 • Fax : +33 1.45.51.81.83
E-mail : editions@lelaurier.fr
www.lelaurier.fr

**Midwest Theological Forum**
1420 Davey Road
Woodridge, IL 60517 U.S.A
Phone: 630 739-9750 • Fax: 630 739-9758
E-mail: mail@mwtf.org